7,00

Making Poetry

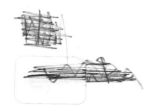

Making Poetry

Approaches to writing
from classrooms
'round the world

by

Brian S. Powell

Collier Macmillan
Canada, Ltd.

Design: Carl Brett
Library of Congress Catalog Card Number
72-92333

02.973440.1 (hardcover)
02.970720.X (paperback)

Collier Macmillan Canada, Ltd.
1125 B Leslie Street, Don Mills, Ontario
Macmillan Publishing Co., Inc.
New York
Printed and Bound in Canada

5 4

79

"The Pickety Fence" © 1952 by David McCord,
from *Far and Few* by David McCord,
by permission of Little, Brown and Co.
and
Reprinted by permission of Curtis Brown Ltd.
© 1925, 1929, 1949, 1950, 1952, 1961,
1962, 1965, 1966, 1967 by David McCord.

Contents

Foreword

There cannot be another book on poetry like this
one, written as it is out of teaching-tours of the
world. The tireless Brian Powell has inspired over
a hundred thousand pupils to write. His method is
a unique method that anyone can learn to use:
proceeding by a structural challenge to say
something personal through the structure. It is a
method that solves that common problem, "How
shall we get started?", for it offers clear patterns
of thought and simple problems to solve, in the
process of which the student finds, often to his
own surprise, that he has something to say. ("How
did I know what I think until I can find a word
form to say it in?")

The students for whom this book is intended are,
in the main, in the age range of nine to fourteen
years. But many of the suggested activities
here are not restricted to any age, simply because
they start out from a precise structure and leave
the theme and level of awareness open. Being
alive, after all, is not exclusive to the ten-year-old,
whatever he may think when he eyes his elders.
The sheer sweat of the search for words is a sweat
that older as well as younger people can well
suffer. Sweating over words is really a struggle
to identify and be vivid about experience. These
pages show what ordinary students can achieve
when a gifted teacher pushes them into the search
for words.

I say gifted teacher and there is no doubt of
Brian Powell's gifts. However, his techniques are
open to anybody who is willing to concentrate
and make his classes concentrate, who enjoys
youthful vision and can convey his enjoyment,
and who is willing in the end to trust the young

spirit. Anyone who does not have these qualities in some measure should not be teaching at all.

Anyone who has a little of them, and would like to cultivate them, will find this book enormously illuminating. Even a gifted teacher finds himself, from time to time, simply *tired,* and he longs for someone to make some suggestions on what to do next. Here he will find an amplitude of such suggestions. If the book is put in the students' hands, they will soon be wanting to do all the exercises themselves. And in the final analysis, teaching is an art directed towards making people want to do it themselves: to write from their own vision, to make language from their own spirit, and to *be* what they have in them to be. Teachers do not give their pupils being. They can only challenge them to dig about in their experience, and so discover and assert their own existence. This book is a rich tool-store for precisely such a digging.

Harold Loukes
Reader in Education
Oxford

Preface

This book could not have grown without the encouragement of many people.

I am most grateful to the principals, heads of departments, and individual teachers of English in hundreds of schools, who have given me a warm welcome and the privilege of working with them.

My particular thanks go to those close friends who have offered me special help: Bill Connell, D'Arcy Coulson, John Clark, Ernie Dinsdale, John Harley, James Peter Jones, Father Jordan, Harold Loukes, David McCord, Père Murray, Bill Oats, Robert Schneider, and Malcolm Stanley.

Young people around the world – over one hundred thousand of them – have shared with me their enthusiasms, their thoughts, and their dreams. To all of them, and especially to those whose writing appears in this book, go my sincere thanks for their inspiration.

And finally, my mother and father, to whose unfailing interest I owe much. To them I dedicate these pages.

B.S.P.

Chapter 1   Introduction
                To
                Poetry Writing

This is a book about teaching and learning. More specifically, it is about English, and the writing of poetry. The ideas contained in it have been developed over the past fifteen years with the help of teachers and pupils in many countries. While it is designed primarily for teachers, the book may also appeal to others who are interested in the thoughts and expression of young people in various parts of the world.

Today, as always, English teaching should try to concentrate on the basic elements of expression: writing, reading, listening, and speaking. At the same time, the use of appropriate words in context should remain at the heart of any study of English. Three concepts are important here. The first of these is *involvement*. Modern approaches to English teaching stress the value of getting pupils actively engaged in group discussions, role playing, project work, use of resource material–in fact, anything that can transform learning from a passive, static process into an active, dynamic one. The Chinese proverb perhaps expresses it best: "I hear and I forget; I see and I remember; I do and I understand".

The second concept is *relevance*. Whatever work is attempted should, as far as possible, be related to the interests and experiences of the pupils themselves. Start from where they are. If they are interested in pop music, or football, or coin collecting, or space travel, or pollution, let them read and write about these things. If topics are meaningful to them, their work is more likely to be lively.

The third concept is *discovery*. In all his work, the teacher of English should be trying to create

situations in which his pupils can discover things
for themselves rather than be told about them.
He should try to give them opportunities to
create on their own and to widen their understanding. This book is designed to help with
this task.

Why Poetry Writing?

Teachers about to start the program may legit-
imately ask: "Why teach English through poetry
writing? What is the background to this approach?
How has it developed?" Initially, the program
grew out of a specific need. My pupils were not
enthusiastic about traditional prose writing. Too
often I found myself asking them to write on
subjects that held little interest for them. In
general they composed loosely, usually to meet
stipulated word totals, and had only scant knowledge of the disciplines required to master their
expression.

Obviously some scheme was required which
would serve to enrich the regular writing program.
It had to provide structural models to help the
pupils develop a sense of form in their writing.
It also had to give them some suggestions about
content (What should they try to write about?)
and evaluation (How might they judge what they
had written?). The result of my thinking was
English Through Poetry Writing. Since publication of the original program, I have heard from
and worked with teachers in many different
countries. They have encouraged me to continue
with the development of its approach, and have
given me suggestions as to how to do so. All the
ideas outlined here have been tested in classrooms with pupils of all levels of ability. While
this book is primarily aimed at pupils from nine

to fourteen years old*, it may be of value to pupils slightly younger or older, depending on their maturity.

What Are Some Of The Factors Involved In Writing?

This question is too complex to be treated in anything short of several volumes, and such a study is not my object here. Let me simply suggest that success in writing may depend, in part at least, on a combination of the following factors:

Control of words While an extensive vocabulary is by no means essential (some of the best writing features simple words), an awareness of the scope of the language is an asset to expression.

Structure A basic knowledge of form, particularly of rhythm and the flow of words, is valuable to any writer.

Content Every writer should realize that he can feed his imagination–his creative heart–through active use of his senses and feelings. This is largely an acquired skill, one that can be nurtured through practice and experience.

Power of concentration Accomplishment in any activity demands the close attention of the participant. Writing is no exception.

Surroundings Where opportunities for concentration exist, as in a well-lit, quiet classroom, the chances of writing success will improve.

Mood of the moment If the writer feels inspired

---

*The author is currently preparing a sequel to this one which will concentrate on the fourteen-to eighteen-year-old range.

at the time of his attempt, he is more likely to produce something that pleases him. He must not expect success at every attempt, however, or be impatient with his own apparent ineptitude.

Desire to write This factor is probably the most important one. If the young person *wants* to write, he should eventually be able to overcome difficulties and achieve satisfaction in his work. Successful writing, in terms of personal satisfaction, depends initially on the willingness of the young person to try and on his determination to try again.

Principles Of The Approach

The program outlined here is based on certain principles and methods of approach. Teachers should understand them before starting, and should apply them, with provisions for individual differences, to their own classrooms.

Classroom Introduction

The period The basic time unit of the program is the individual English period. Much of the writing takes place within it, in addition to group discussion of the work produced. A typical period involves a five- to ten-minute introduction by the teacher, followed by twenty minutes of writing by the pupils, and concludes with ten to fifteen minutes of reading and group discussion. This format should be open to considerable variation, however. On some days the whole period might be devoted to the reading of work produced in a previous session. On others it might be given to hearing pieces the pupils have written outside class. Basically, however, the class period is the time when the teacher introduces an idea and gives his pupils a chance to start developing it.

The formula The teacher has ten minutes in which to get his pupils involved in an idea. In his introduction he should propose some shape or structure for the piece, suggest a topic for the day, and read several pieces done by other pupils as illustrations of the topic. He should present a definite objective to the pupils in his introduction, one that offers them direction as well as freedom to use their own thoughts and interests. Younger or less experienced pupils will usually benefit from a more tightly structured introduction. Too much freedom of choice at too early a stage only leads to confusion. Consider the following three factors of the introduction:

Form Beginners will benefit from some suggestions about form. They should be introduced to a wide range of forms, starting with ones which are tightly controlled and progressing to those which are freer in structure. In the early stages of the course the pupil should experiment with a range of forms which will serve as the foundation for his further expression.

Content Pupils should be encouraged to write on topics that are of interest to them. They should be brought to realize that anything is "grist to the writer's mill," and that their own experiences provide the best base from which to start. However, in the initial stages the teacher should make content suggestions. Pupils who are just beginning to write poetry have little idea of focus, and given free choice often pick topics that are too difficult or inappropriate for them.*

Examples After discussing form and content with his pupils, the teacher should read them several

*See the introduction to specific items, chapter 3, page 33, for further detail on this point.

examples of the idea for the day, preferably from the work of other young writers. These examples should be carefully chosen to illustrate the aim of the exercise, without being so powerful as to place the pupils in a mental strait jacket. For instance, if the teacher reads a forceful piece criticizing school food, it may trigger other anti-school protests which probably would not have arisen otherwise. At its best, an example should provide direction without restricting individual freedom of thought.

Classroom Atmosphere

Silence The act of writing is an individual, not a shared experience. Hence the teacher should ask for quiet in the classroom so that each pupil can concentrate on his own work. Experience shows that the time for discussion and exchange of ideas is after, not during the actual writing. Silence during the writing session–and hence the opportunity to concentrate–is perhaps the most important factor contributing to the success of each pupil.

Concentration The teacher should emphasize that in order to do anything well–play a sport, sew on a button, fry an egg, or write a poem–one must concentrate on what one is doing. The pupil should be trained to devote his full attention to his writing, even if only for short periods of time. Once he learns to do so (and this is partly a function of maturity as well as effort) he should be able to escape in mind from the four walls of the classroom. The mind is capable of almost anything if we give it flight on the wings of concentration.

Understanding While writing itself is an individual experience, the reading and discussion of work can be a shared one. The teacher should encourage his pupils to be understanding toward the efforts of their classmates. They should be taught that learning to write is a skill which is difficult to master and at which nobody achieves perfection. If pupils hesitate to write what they honestly feel because of a fear of the mockery of others, then the climate for creative accomplishment will be unsatisfactory. The teacher should nurture an atmosphere of understanding and encouragement in the classroom, and take action if some of his pupils do not recognize the importance of this factor.

Creative tension No one should be deluded into thinking that this program seeks to produce instant poetry. Just trying to write does not guarantee success. Professional writers know this. Experience shows, however, that a certain positive tension is generated in any situation where a group assembles in the hope of creating something. The very urgency of the situation, the time limit imposed by the class period itself, often serves as a stimulus, particularly to those who, faced with no pressure whatsoever, would probably produce nothing.

Attitude Of The Teacher

Confidence The teacher must eventually develop confidence in the program, the pupils, and himself. Confidence will come with time and experience. He should not try to "sell" the approach, but rather let the involvement of his pupils produce its own impact. However, he should try to write poetry himself. Every teacher of English should be a practising writer as well. In this way he experiences the joys and frustrations of creation along with his pupils.

Potential An experienced teacher of art whom
I know made this statement: "Every pupil who
comes into my room has the potential to create
art. My job is to provide him with paints,
brushes, canvas–the materials for his work. If
he has problems with technique, if he wants to
know how to draw a particular line, or mix a
particular colour, then I try to teach him the
skills involved. Otherwise, I stand out of his
way." The teacher of English should operate in a
similar way. He should try to teach his pupils
techniques of expression as the need arises
from the work they are doing. Otherwise he
should encourage them to write, and then let
them go ahead without interference.

Encouragement The beginning writer probably
lacks confidence, and will benefit from the
encouragement of his teacher. This encouragement must not be false praise. On the other
hand, there are few pieces of writing, that have
no redeeming features. Let the teacher emphasize
the positive, rather than the negative aspects of
the work. He might offer incentives for good
writing, such as display on the notice board,
publication in a class newspaper, or recommen-
dation to the principal. Encouragement serves as
a stimulus for continued effort.

Flexibility Every teacher should be sensitive to
the individual needs and interests of his pupils.
The approach proposed in this book is not an
inflexible formula, but a series of ideas which
should be adapted by teachers to their own situations. For example, projects which captivate
pupils living in country areas may be inappropriate to those in the inner city. Similarly, suggestions which appeal to the imagination and
style of one teacher may be of little interest to
another. Each teacher should try to develop the

ability to "take the pulse" of his own classroom situation. He must then be flexible in adapting the suggestions made here to provide for it.

Writing Procedure

Ideas book Many experienced writers of poetry–men like Robert Graves, Stephen Spender and Ted Hughes–keep an "ideas book". This is a notebook carried for the purpose of recording thoughts, experiences, or ideas as they occur and before they can be forgotten. The book contains jottings which serve as the foundations for later writing. Each pupil should keep a similar book. He will benefit from the discipline of recording events and experiences, and at the same time he will be accumulating a storehouse of ideas which will be valuable when he comes to write. He should bring his ideas book to each writing session.

Exercise book Teachers should ask their pupils to keep an exercise book for writing. This book serves as a record both of work in progress and of completed pieces. Each left-hand page is used as a draft sheet. The first version, as well as all subsequent alterations, are recorded here. When making changes the pupil can simply cross out, not erase completely, so that he has a progressive record of the development of his idea. The right-hand page is used for completed pieces. Before the writer re-copies his finished work onto the right-hand page, he should verify mechanical details such as spelling, grammar, and punctuation which, if left uncorrected, would spoil the finished product.

Re-writing This is the heart of the creative enterprise, the essential stage without which few pieces achieve their potential. Pupils must realize that

achieving effective expression requires a knowledge of certain skills, considerable experience,
and most important, sustained hard work.

Expectations: Questions And Answers

In this concluding section let me try to anti-
cipate and answer some of your questions. I
hope that you will write to me personally with
others that may arise from your own
experience.

Q. Can the ordinary teacher of English, with no
   special background in creative writing, suc-
   cessfully carry out this program?

A. Many have, and more are continuing to do
   so. Just be yourself, believe in your pupils,
   and make a start. If you have done your
   homework, and if you try yourself to write
   on the topic you are giving your class, you
   should quickly gain confidence. Before long,
   you and your class will be devising your
   own original forms and suggestions.

Q. Can any pupil, regardless of ability, derive
   benefit from this program? Or is its value
   limited to pupils with greater creative
   ability?

A. Any pupil willing to make a concentrated
   effort can receive pleasure and benefit from
   this program. Each pupil will profit from it
   in a different way. Experience shows that
   pupils who are supposed to be less able,
   according to their ratings on standard intel-
   ligence tests, frequently succeed at creative
   work. On the other hand, they are often
   frustrated by more formal academic assign-
   ments. Their writing often contains an originality and freshness not found in the work
   of supposedly "brighter" pupils.

Q. How frequently should poetry-writing periods be held?

A. Experience shows that a creative session held once every week or ten days is sufficient to establish the value of the program. You must recognize that the poetry writing is proposed as an addition to the regular language teaching. It does not replace or eliminate anything already being done, but serves as an enrichment to the language work. As such, it should not be overused.

Q. Should creative writing be marked?

A. It is to be hoped that educational systems everywhere are swinging away from exclusively *quantitative* assessments (where a pupil is given a mark out of one hundred, for example,) toward *qualitative* ones, where constructive comments are more imporant than raw scores. Pupils like to be rewarded when they give their best efforts to any task. Consequently, you should try to strike a balance between remarks and marks. There are certain standards of expression which you can use as an objective basis for constructive criticism of a work.* However, you should not pass judgment on the overall quality of a pupil. Your major concern should be to encourage your pupils, and help them to improve their writing by trying to teach them the skills of expression.

Q. How much completed writing should the teacher realistically expect to result from any creative session?

---

*John Clark, an English master at Winchester College, England, is currently working on a book entitled *Legitimate Questions* which should be of considerable value to teachers in English.

A. Don't try to judge the success of any writing period on the basis of work produced on the spot. Most professional writers don't try, or aren't able, to "write to order". Why, then, should we expect pupils to do so? The result of any writing period should more realistically be measured in terms of interest generated and ideas set in motion. It is the quality of time shared that helps to determine the amount of creative activity to occur subsequently. The writing period is for planting; the harvest may not come till later.

Q. Is the program concerned exclusively with the writing of poetry, or does it have wider application to other forms of expression?

A. One could dwell at length on definitions of terms (What is poetry anyway?) and be little the wiser at the end of the exercise. This program is concerned with words and their appropriate use *whatever* the form: descriptive paragraphs, expositional essays, business letters, short stories, examinations, character sketches, mood pieces, and so on. The important thing is that pupils become familiar with the language, and hence able to make words work for them. Poetic forms are used as one of the many possible means to the end of more effective expression.

Q. Does the poetry-writing program integrate with the rest of the work in the subject we call English?

A. It should. If a pupil has tried to write some poetry himself, he has a better understanding of the craft of the poet, and hence a closer link with the formal poets he studies in the literature part of his course.* There are other advantages as well. Once a pupil has written and then re-worked his own pieces, he has experience with functional grammar, spelling and syntax. His powers of observation are sharpened through the discipline of trying to write poetry, and this skill helps him with other forms of writing. And finally, having tried to share his own thoughts and experiences with others, he should have a better concept of what literature is about.

Q. Are there any difficulties for the beginning teacher in using this approach?

A. Not really. The program is not proposed as a blueprint to be followed to the letter. You must experiment with it and establish procedures that are appropriate to your own pupils. A combination of professional skill, common sense, and concern for your pupils should help to overcome any problems that arise. As you grow in understanding, so also will the program.

---

*It is to be hoped that pupils who have gained some knowledge of the technique of writing poetry may *want* to read Wordsworth, Robert Frost, Judith Wright, or other recognized writers.

Chapter 2

Approaches To Form I:

Forms Which Emphasize The Single Word

One morning as I approached a school, I saw a class of ten-year-olds outside in the garden. They were having an art class. Each pupil held in his hand at arm's length from his eyes a piece of cardboard which had a small square cut in the centre of it. As I watched, they moved these pieces of cardboard across the landscape, and looked intently through the frames in the centre. Their teacher knew that young artists, given no guidelines, will probably try to put the whole world onto their canvases. Their work will lack focus. To avoid this problem he had instructed each pupil to look through the cardboard frame, discover there a subject that appealed to him, and then to put what he had in his view-finder – and *only* what he had there – into his picture. The frame provided the form or structure for the painting.

A parallel exists in writing. Beginners will benefit from some guidance with form. Otherwise their expression may lack focus, and hence precision and direction. Experience indicates that a progression of forms, starting from the tightly structured, and moving toward the freer, will provide the pupil with the most useful background.

This chapter presents a number of suggestions about form which should be of value to young writers in developing their skills of expression. While they are intended chiefly for those in the nine- to fourteen-year-old age range, they should also prove useful as exercises for older writers.*

---

*It is worth remembering in this connection that most concert pianists still spend several hours a day practising scales.

You should select the items for presentation to
your class in the order you believe most suitable.
Once you are familiar with the approach, you
and your pupils should be able to devise your
own forms to add to those proposed here.

What Is It?

The heart of any expression lies in picking
the appropriate word for a given context.
The first model should help to illustrate
this point. Let each pupil select a subject,
anything he is interested in and knows
something about. Let him then write about
it, using as many of the five senses - taste,
touch, smell, sight, sound - as he can apply to
his subject. He is allowed only one word,
probably an adjective, to describe each
sense, and he withholds the title until the
final line. Thus his poem has the following
framework:

Sight	_____
Sound	_____
Taste	_____
Touch	_____
Smell	_____
Subject	_____

The pupil may rearrange the order of senses
to suit his subject. After he has written his
piece, the other pupils should try to guess
his subject. If he has written accurately,
they should be able to guess correctly. If
some of his adjectives are inappropriate, confusion will result. Consider the following examples:

red
smoky
crackling
hot
fire.

(P.R., Friends School,
Hobart, Australia)

sour
yellow
crunchy
sticky
lemon life-saver.

(P.G., Outremont High School,
Montreal, Canada)

slimy
goggling
croaking
frogs.

(M.P., Taroona High School,
Taroona, Australia)

bouncy
fruit-tasting
crystal
soundless
Jell-o.

(M.T., Riverdale High School,
Montreal, Canada)

red
crackly
curld
dry
levs.*

(D.P., Dalton School
for Spastics, New Town,
Australia)

* This poem is reproduced exactly as written on his typewriter by a
twelve-year-old spastic boy.

round
sour
juicy
lemon.

(M.V., Pius X High School,
Montreal, Canada)

The piece on "lemon" perhaps best illustrates the value of this form. The young
writer who produced it speaks Italian as a
mother tongue, and doesn't have a wide
English vocabulary. When she read her
piece to the class, most of the other pupils,
in trying to guess the subject, said
"grapefruit." The writer soon realized that
her selection of the word "round" was
incorrect. She realized that "oval" was the
word she needed.

Three-Word Model

Ask the pupils to make a three-word piece
with the following pattern:

Noun   _____
Verb   _____
Adverb   _____

Each of the three parts of speech must start
with the same letter. This provides the piece
with a unifying thread through sound.
Obviously, then, the first letter of the noun
determines the first letter of the verb and
adverb. In introducing this model to younger
pupils, you have the opportunity to present
a functional grammar lesson. If the pupils
don't know what an adverb is, they must
find out before they are able to write the
piece. This is perhaps one way to make a

study of parts of speech meaningful to young writers.

You should also emphasize the skill involved in picking the most appropriate adverb. Look at this example:

masters
meditate
m_____ly

(J.K., Sydney Grammar School, Sydney, Australia)

The writer must select an adverb that best suits the tone and intention of his piece. Through it he will be trying to transmit his attitude and point of view. In this case, the boy was about to face an important exam and he felt glum. Hence an adverb such as "merrily" was not appropriate to his mood. He thought of "maliciously", but felt this word was too strong for what he wanted to say. As he wanted to give the piece a tone of tongue-in-cheek humour, he finally decided on the adverb "menacingly", which seems appropriate for his intention.*

This example shows that picking a word to fit a context demands thought and discrimination. Experience should make the task of the young writers easier. Here are several other examples of this model:

spiders
spin
speechlessly

(D.L., Mt. St. Benedict's School, Sydney, Australia)

*See chapter 4, page 86, for a further example of this type.

slugs
slide
slimily

(E.P., J.F. Kennedy High School,
Montreal, Canada)

porcupines
prickle
painfully

(D.T., Phillips Exeter
Academy, Exeter, U.S.A.)

gorillas
growl
grumpily

(T.V., Riverdale High School,
Montreal, Canada)

sonar
sweeps
searchingly

(J.B., John Rennie High School,
Montreal, Canada)

tanks
trudge
tirelessly

(L.S., Repton School,
Derbyshire, England)

Pupils who become enthusiastic about this
form might try to produce one model for
every letter of the alphabet.

Cinquain

Another form which encourages accuracy
of word usage is an adaptation of the
classical cinquain. In this exercise the young
writer is asked to follow this model:

————,

————, ————,

————, ————, ————,

———— ———— ———— ————,

————

In the diagram the first line is a single word, the subject. It may be anything that interests the pupil. The second line contains two adjectives, both describing the subject, unrelated structurally, and separated by a comma. The third line contains three adjectives, again unrelated. The fourth line contains four words forming a phrase or clause, connected grammatically and in sense. The final line simply repeats the subject. The cinquain provides a definite and achievable pattern, and should spark a wide range of pieces.

hamburgers,
thick, juicy,
delicious, scrumptious, yummy,
better still with relish,
hamburgers.

(M.L., Dunton High School,
Montreal, Canada)

alley cat,
slinking, stinking,
bony, scraggy, sly,
evil but with grace,
alley cat.

(C.J., Friends School,
Hobart, Australia)

desert,
hot, sandy,
sweaty, thirsty, treeless,
bitter cold at night,
desert.

(A.G., Scots College,
Warwick, Australia)

hair,
long, shiny,
thick, curly, healthy,
grow and never stop,
hair.

(E.S., Montreal West High School,
Montreal, Canada)

noise,
insistent, persistent,
banging, clatterring, crashing,
reverberating in my head,
noise.

(J.T., Raffles Institution,
Singapore)*

girls,
beautiful, affectionate,
36, 24, 36,
bring them to me,
girls.

(J.G., Outremont High School,
Montreal, Canada)

hawk,
powerful, free,
soaring, swooping, sailing,
always searching for prey,
hawk.

(S.C., Lyndon Institute,
Lyndonville, U.S.A.)

The cinquain also offers scope for experiment with sound, as the example on "hawk" illustrates. Read it again aloud.

Form Poem: Two-Words

In the early stages of the program rhyme can prove a barrier to many young writers. You should only insist on rhyme when you are trying to show that sound is a basic element of poetry and rhyme is an element of sound.

---

* Mr. John Tan is the Head of the English Department at Singapore's premier school. He wrote this poem with his students in the busy heart of downtown Singapore.

Ask the pupils to try a piece with the following pattern:

```
————— , ————— ,
————— ,   A   ,
————— , ————— ,
—————     A
```

Each verse of this model has four lines, each comprising two words, with the second and fourth lines rhyming (A's above). In the first three lines the words chosen are not grammatically related, but they must be appropriate to the subject and contribute to its development. In the fourth line the two words must be grammatically related; thus they are not separated by commas as are the words in the first three lines.

Pupils may pick any subject they wish–narrative or humourous pieces are often popular–but they must concentrate on picking the most appropriate words they can think of. Here are several examples of this model:

Vietnam
Jungle, swamp,
sweat, heat,
hunger, thirst,
Tired feet.

Bunks, bombs,
mortar, shell,
thoughts, home,
Living hell.
(J.F.,* Monklands High School,
Montreal, Canada)

* I am grateful to Jane Eddison, a pupil at Monklands High School, for
  her suggestion of this model.

Summer Traffic Jam
Hot, slow,
sun, glare,
stop, start,
Tempers flare.
(L.C., Iolani School,
Honolulu, Hawaii)

Skiing I
Skis, poles,
St. Bernard, keg,
snow, wind,
broken leg.

Skiing II
Mountain, cliff,
speedy, fast,
exhilarating, fun,
hardened cast.
(B.M., West Hill High School,
Montreal, Canada)

Blindness
Dreary, black,
afraid, alone,
voices, empty,
steps unknown.
(L.S., Hutchins School,
Hobart, Australia)

First Driving Lesson
Teacher, shout,
light, red,
policeman, ticket,
driver's ed.
(J.P., St. Johnsbury Academy,
St. Johnsbury, U.S.A.)

Five-Line Adjective-Verb Model

Another model emphasizing parts of speech
is illustrated by the following poem:

The sun on snow looks
glassy,
glossy;
It glistens,
gleams.

(L.C., West Hill High School,
Montreal, Canada)

This is a five-line model in which the writer establishes any situation he wishes to in the first line. Probably some type of description will suit best. The second and third lines are single adjectives, both beginning with the same letter and chosen for their appropriateness. The fourth line comprises a pronoun and a verb, the fifth line a verb only. The verbs of the fourth and fifth lines begin with the same letter as the two adjectives above, so that all four lines begin with the same *sound*. Consequently, before he begins to write the pupil should carefully consider what sound is associated with the subject he has chosen.

This form encourages the pupil to think about his subject in detail, and even to explore a thesaurus to select the adjectives and verbs that will help make his subject come alive.

Eel
The eel on the hook feels
slimy,
scummy;
It stretches,
shrinks.

(M.C., Lyndon Institute,
Lyndonville, U.S.A.)

Sky
The sky at night looks
silky,
silent;
It shivers,
sheens.

(P.V., Macdonald High School,
St. Anne de Bellevue, Canada)

Hawk
The hawk in flight looks
deadly,
dangerous;
It dips,
dives.

(I.K., Normanhurst Boys' High School,
Sydney, Australia)

Gloved Hand
A leather-gloved hand feels
smooth,
spongey;
It soothes,
stimulates.

(V.L., Crown Woods Comprehensive School,
London, England)

Three-Line Location-Action Model

Ask young writers to do a three-line piece with
the following general framework:

First line: the subject (in a word or two)
Second line: the location of the subject (in a
phrase or clause)
Third line: action of the subject (briefly)

The exact number of words in each of the lines
need not matter as long as the expression is
concise. The well-written piece should be
almost like a verbal slide. It presents a moment
in time, frozen in words.

The Lone One
The tree,
On a lone pinnacle,
Stands.

(T.M., Carmel High School, Carmel, U.S.A.)

Chamois*
Les chamois,
Au sommets des monts,
Se battent.

(W.F., École Primaire de Val d'Isère, Savoie, France)

Barracuda
The barracuda,
In the water,
Pries into conch shells.

(F.M., Public School,
Harbour Island, Bahamas)

Dingo
A dingo,
Silhouetted against the sky,
Bays.

(R.B., Sydney Grammar School,
Sydney, Australia)

Pupils might also try to make a piece which contains several verses of three-line construction. Such a piece would probably have a strong narrative emphasis.

"I Wish" Model

Let the pupils think about things they would like. Have them start with single lines ("I wish I could travel in a space capsule") and then put a number of wishes together to make a poem. With beginners or with those who use English as a second language this exercise works well as a class project. Each pupil contributes

* translation - *Chamois* (Mountain goat)
  The Chamois
  On the peaks of the mountains
  Fight

a single line, and the teacher builds the
completed poem on the board.

Here are two examples. The second one was
written by a young Portuguese boy who had
only recently arrived in Montreal and was on the
threshold of his first Canadian winter.

I wish when I go fishing I wouldn't lose my bait;
I wish I had two birthdays;
I wish I played hockey like Bobby Orr;*
I wish I could finish my homework in five minutes;
I wish I could make this last line rhyme;
I wish that my wishes would come true.

(D.B., John Grant High School,
Montreal, Canada)

I wish when I go bowling, the ball would go the
    right way;
I wish I had the brain of a computer to pass my
    tests;
I wish I could talk to my friend in *his* language;
I wish I had a bicycle that wasn't broken;
I wish it was hotter outside today.

(E.P., Our Lady of Mt. Royal School,
Montreal, Canada)

The "Now Experience"

At every moment of the day our senses are
bombarded with various experiences: sights,
sounds, smells, touch sensations, and tastes.
In addition to sense experiences, we also
undergo emotional ones: moods, feelings,
reactions. Ask your pupils to concentrate on
their experiences of the present moment. They
must write, as precisely and completely as they
are able, about the thoughts, feelings and sense

---

* Bobby Orr is the young Canadian superstar who plays hockey for the
  Boston Bruins.

experiences that come to them in the next sixty seconds. They must try to record their own "now experience". Have them put down their feelings as single completed lines. Those who are living with intensity should develop a reasonable number of lines, even within the short period of time allotted.

This exercise has the obvious benefit of encouraging each young person to observe his world and himself more carefully. Teachers must be quick to guarantee their pupils a type of "writer's immunity". Nothing that a pupil says should be held against him; otherwise he won't write what he really feels, and the exercise will lose some of its value.

Any number of interesting observations may emerge:

Now I feel the wind cooling the perspiration
on my brow.
I feel like flying around the room like that wasp.
Now I hear a bus coming up the drive in low
gear.
My head throbs as if I'd just run into a brick
wall.
I feel like shouting out loud for joy.
I want to punch that fellow in the nose.

This exercise is a catalyst. Its aim is to stimulate observation and expression.

Unit About a Theme

In preparing the young writer to do slightly longer pieces, you should emphasize the importance of unity. A poem, or any form of writing, must be held together by a unifying strand or idea. Beginners, in particular, tend to ramble unless they learn the principle of unity. Ask the pupils to think of any simple

topic, and then to diagram their pieces before
they begin formal writing. The topic *At the game*
is diagrammed below:

Any detail that is included must have some
direct bearing on the topic. It must not be
included if it does not logically belong.
Developing unity is largely a matter of
organization. Once the pupil has decided on
and organized the details of his topic, he may
proceed to write his piece.

Chapter 3   Approaches
To
Content

The previous chapter presented suggestions to help the young writer with *form*. Specific structures were introduced as the framework for his ideas, and he was asked to write to these structures much as an artist might be asked to paint on canvases of different specific sizes.

Pupils might also benefit from some suggestions on *content*. The approaches to content proposed in this chapter are universal in that they may be used by any pupil regardless of his age. He need only bring his own experiences to each suggestion. The young person who is observant and conscious of things around him will probably find writing easier than the person who is not. There is truth to the saying: "Originality is a good pair of eyes".

Choosing A Topic

If pupils inexperienced in writing are given a completely open choice of topic ("write about *anything* you want") they are frequently confused. As beginners they have little concept of *focus*. For example, take the two topics *fire* and *flame*. At first glance, the beginner probably feels they are roughly the same. He may not realize that *fire* is a general noun that can refer to a variety of things: a bush fire, a burning building, a big or small blaze. *Flame,* on the other hand, is much more specific. It has focus. The writer gets a definite visual image when he thinks about flame; he can almost see licking tongues of orange, red, and yellow. For this reason *flame* is a more appropriate topic and in the majority of cases will yield a more satisfactory result to the writer.

An important element of focus lies in the choice

of the singular or plural. A plural focus
generally gives an indefinite visual image.
Consider the topic *fenceposts,* for example.
It gives a visual impression of a great many
fenceposts extending into the horizon. No
single one stands out. However, if one considers
the singular focus, *fencepost,* a definite image
jumps to the mind's eye, perhaps grey and
splintered, trailing barbed-wire, or protruding
from an unruly clump of grass.

It should be obvious from the examples above
that pupils generally benefit from some carefully chosen suggestions from their teacher.
Read them a list of, say, fifteen different
topics, and ask them to write about the one
that interests them most. Give them the option
to choose their own topic only if they don't like
any of the items you suggest.*

You must work to devise lists of topics which
are suitable and attractive to your pupils.** It
is not appropriate to ask pupils in the interior
of Australia to write about icicles nor students
in the heart of a big city to write about
African wild animals. They probably won't
know very much about them, and so should be
given topics more related to their own
experience.

Here are a number of lists with which I have
been working lately. They may serve as a
starting point. The area in which these topics
have been used is affixed to each list. In the

*Experience shows that less than two per cent of pupils do, in fact,
make up their own.

**The pupils themselves are an excellent source of inspiration in making
up these lists.

case of the Australian lists, I have also attached a number to each topic which represents the number of pupils who, given completely free choice of all fifteen, picked that particular one.*

North American list

seaweed	wind
neon light	cactus
haystack	sea shell
bark	trailer truck
slush	worm
flame	smoke
brick	burr
icicle	mud
fire hydrant	bubble
snowdrift	motorbike
blade of grass	skyscraper
cobweb	oilslick
tar	telegraph pole
fence post	pebble
scarecrow	cigar butt

soap	
twig	pearl
bulldozer	smokestack
chrome	boxcar
fog	bee
pumpkin	sunbeam
wave	pigeon
ant	lightning

*These figures were obtained during a two-month teaching-tour to all parts of Australia in 1971. They are included here strictly for interest value. I make no attempt to estimate *why* pupils pick the topics they do. If an item does not prove of some interest, reject it and replace it.

Hawaiian list

sunset	
sandals	broken glass
coconut	construction crane
shark	dying flower
banana split	sunshine
waterfall	sand crab
mango	rainbow
surf	brown paper bag

Australian lists

I

neon light	45
sunset	113
broken glass	89
hamburger	34
dripping tap	41
toothpaste	59
burnt grass	36
gum tree	46
flame	93
bleaching bones	33
surf	116
oilslick	47
orange peel	28
spider web	48
dust storm	54
	(approx. 900)

II

traffic	131
sunrise	134
spider	82
rubbish tip	114
guitar	27
seaweed	75
signpost	73

meat pie	30
candle	41
pantihose	46
clock	37
motorbike	74
smokestack	36
tinfoil	28
sweat	62
	(approx. 1000)

III
ink blotch	52
speedboat	47
mini-skirt	125
barbed wire	127
snake	121
skyscraper	49
dead fish	116
traffic light	34
cicada	27
smog	132
suntan oil	45
hawk	56
milk shake	37
driftwood	55
tar	85
	(approx. 1100)

IV
jeans	71
lamp post	101
dragster	44
aquarium	42
paddle-pop stick	54
light bulb	51
sheep dog	56
cigarette butt	74
thunder cloud	66
chewing gum	184

weed	41
rubbish bin	82
possum	32
mud	71
candy wrapper	25
	(approx. 1000)

V

fallen leaf	139
litter box	68
jellyfish	124
Kentucky-fried chicken	54
beard	46
bikini	94
crumpled tin can	59
sunburn	80
freeway	46
ice cube	71
rotten fruit	41
dust	100
alley cat	60
tree stump	48
worm	107
	(approx. 1100)

VI

park bench	67
ice cream cone	64
concrete pavement	65
swagman	100
anchor	62
mongrel	46
puncture	36
surf	80
squeaking gate	53
jumbo jet	45
scribble	51
beach buggy	61

bubbler   42
rusty metal   46
ping-pong ball   100
                        (approx. 900)

Singapore lists

I

high rise flats	overhead bridge
coconut	pasa malam (night market)
trishaw	chinese opera
chilly crabs	monkey
satay (skewered meat)	traffic jam
sampan man	durian (nut-like fruit)
orchid	heat
ants	

II

rambutan (fruit)	kite
lion dance	mosquitoes
spectacles	noodles
waterfront	bullock cart
chopsticks	rain
puppet	rubber tree
moon	Chinatown
Kampong (Malay village)	

East African lists

I

ostrich	poacher
Masai (native tribe)	film
rift valley	herdsman
waterbuck	national park
Saturday shopping	wind
changaa (national drink)	Mt. Kenya
ugali (maize porridge)	lion
wood carvings	

II

maize	banga (drink)
red soil	bird sanctuary
uhuru (independence)	safari van
Kilimanjaro	giraffe
coffee	turkana (hunter)
snake	Tree Tops Reserve
sales kiosk	spear

harambee (slogan meaning "working together")

United Kingdom lists

I

cabbage	washing line
hovercraft	double-decker bus
cathedral	gypsy camp
badger	cricket pitch
cracker	Chelsea boots
hedge	seagull
strawberries	beech woods
bobby (policeman)	

II

potato patch	Cup final
hedgehog	antique shop
sailing	hops
toffee apple	Rolls Royce
castle ruins	village green
pub	orchard
fog	Marks and Spencer
level crossing	

III

stained-glass window	cornfield
go-kart	vintage car

fish 'n' chips
street lamp
umbrella
vest-pocket gold watch
poplar tree
soccer ball

bowler hat
tea
Big Ben
white cliffs
lemonade

Content Conciseness

Once you have read the list of topics, ask the pupils to pick a topic and write about it in four lines or less. A major aim of this exercise is conciseness. Each pupil should try to make his poem what the Chinese call "trimmed to the bone"*, eliminating all unnecessary verbiage. Impact in writing is usually achieved by hitting the nail directly on the head. Here are a few examples of this idea. Every teacher should keep a collection of the pieces his own pupils produce.

Swagman
Wandering, roaming,
Just whiskers, skin and bone,
Out on the dusty trail
All alone.

(P.D., Brisbane Grammar School,
Brisbane, Australia)

Boxcar
The rust-red boxcar stands idle on the siding;
It stands for days:
Its brake lines limp,
Its knuckles stiff and cold.

(D.O., Phillips Exeter Academy,
Exeter, U.S.A.)

* From Arthur Waley's translations of Chinese poetry found in the anthology *The White Pony*.

Broken Glass
Glittering in the sand,
The reject;
Waiting for revenge,
Silent.

(D.F., Riverview College,
Sydney, Australia)

Slush
Soft, soggy slush,
Sitting all alone;
Filling up with grit,
Uugghh...slush.

(A.M., Fleming School,
Brandon, Canada)

Concrete Waterfall
Concrete waterfall,
Stone and glass,
Doesn't seem to fall;
Just goes up, touching the sky.

(S.M., Iolani School,
Honolulu, Hawaii)

Sunburn
Hot, red and sore all over;
Burning,
Burning right into your skin,
Too sore to do anything.

(L.B., Coogee South Public School,
Sydney, Australia)

Scribble
A child's view of life
Messed and jotted
On a wall.

(L.R., Bathurst Demonstration School,
Bathurst, Australia)

Mini-skirt
What skirt?
Is that a skirt?
Are you sure it's a skirt?
Wow.

(T.P., Raffles Institution, Singapore)

Jumbo Jet
A flying whale, clumsy,
Thirty-two rubber feet–so sure footed;
So strong–to carry so many;
So gentle–to land so softly.
(M.C., Sydney Grammar School,
Sydney, Australia)

Fence Post
Desolate,
Caught in barbed wire;
Standing tall–
A guard.
(L.G., St. George's School,
Vancouver, Canada)

Fish
Submerged scaly flashes,
Gleaming.
(N.B., St. Edmund's School,
Canterbury, England)

Hedgehog
Four stumpy legs,
Thousands of prickles;
A long snout–
Hedgehog.
(R.W., Foremark School,
Derbyshire, England)

Meaning Through Observation

One of the skills that every writer must eventually develop is the ability to give significance to seemingly trivial things. He must also see relationships between apparently unrelated items: a butterfly on a stone, a pigeon waddling, apples with snow on them. The writer learns to give meaning to such everyday experiences through attention to details that escape the unobservant. Thus an experienced writer frequently expresses an insight which almost everyone has had, but does not realize until he sees it in words. Ask the pupils to write a short

piece which highlights any insight they have
gained by making a relationship between previously unrelated things.

Fire Hydrant
The fire hydrant
Was not meant
For dogs.
But I have found
The dogs around
Frequently.
(W.B., Phillips Exeter Academy,*
Exeter, U.S.A.)

Spring
Until the spring of my thirteenth year
When I heard the songbirds,
I neither stopped, nor listened:
Now I recognize the spring
Not by the weather,
But by the songs.
(E.M., Wagar High School, Montreal, Canada)

Elms
Elm trees have black dying fingers
That cut the sky.
Some have white plaques nailed on their trunks
That say, 'Dutch Elm disease suspect.'
(T.F., Henley Grammar School, Henley, England)

Rose
Down the seed falls;
Up the rose climbs,
Soundless–
With all its effort
Grasping for the sky.
(S.S., Hull Elementary School, Hull, Canada)

Autumn
We walked through the forest
All through the day,

---

* I am grateful for this example to Jack Heath, a distinguished teacher
  of English at Exeter. It was written by William Beckleau, a former
  pupil of his at the academy.

Gathering leaves of many colours:
On our way home,
We realized that
We had autumn in our pockets.
(D.M., Verdun High School, Montreal, Canada)

Pain
I fear to feel
Pain;
For my heart is not of stone,
And bleeds
When touched unkindly.
(M.B., Santa Sabena School, Sydney, Australia)

Morning
The crowing of the rooster
Breaks open the lonesome peace
Of morning.
(L.L., Msgr. Doran School, Montreal, Canada)

Pine Tree
Look.
The tree has been crying amber teardrops;
Perhaps it has a soul.
(T.S., Punahou School, Honolulu, Hawaii)

Travel
Go to a room;
Sit in a chair;
Close your eyes tight-
Travel somewhere.
(K.C., St. John's School, Selkirk, Canada)

Nature As Content

Nature in all its varied elements and faces
seems to hold a fascination for young people
the world over. Interest in plants, trees, insects,
birds, and rocks appears to be universal. Ask
the pupils to write about anything from
nature, preferably something they have not
previously considered. It might be a very small,
or seemingly insignifigant item, such as an

ant, a pebble, or a blade of grass.* In attempting their piece, they should try to avoid the trite and the conventional. You might find it useful to speak about clichés and hackneyed expression in this regard.

To those with open eyes and ears the world of nature offers an ever-changing source of inspiration.

Kookaburra
A wonder wizard of the sky,
Raucous, rowdy, raging;
Gulping gasps of pure fresh air,
A drunkard of the heavens.

(G.W., Riverview College, Sydney, Australia)

February Ski Trail
Twigs,
Dead leaves,
And sticks so bare,
Lying on the crust,
Lifeless;
Yet suggesting spring,
And green,
And growth again.

(B.P., Putney School, Putney, U.S.A.)

Low Tide
Half-rotten coconut,
Crazily jumping fish,
Retreating tinted crab,
Watersnakes,
Smell–
Low tide in a mangrove swamp.

(J.S., Friends School, Hobart, Australia)*

**Caterpillars
Caterpillars dance
Slowly, slowly,

---

* The poetry of Walter de la Mare might be useful to the teacher in emphasizing the treatment of "small" subjects.

** The pupil who wrote this piece had just enjoyed a holiday in New Caledonia, and had been captivated by the waterfront there.

Stepping in time
To the Go-Go.
(M.M., Bathurst Demonstration School, Bathurst,
Australia)

Raindrops after Dark
Silently they drop
From a sickly red sky,
These evening raindrops,
Sparkling on leaf tips,
Glistening on the street.
(K.U., Raffles Institution, Singapore)

Pine Tree
Pine Tree–
Tall and thin,
Swaying,
Bending,
Dropping needles on the ground;
Turning,
Twisting,
Whistling in the wind–
Pine Tree.
(D.R., Carmel High School, Carmel, U.S.A.)

Fish
Fish–
Corrugated shimmers,
Bubbles.
(L.W., Woolhara School, Sydney, Australia)

Seeds
Seeds,
Decaying,
Swaying on tall stalks,
In the wind–
Fragile.
(M.P., Punahou School, Honolulu, Hawaii)

The Soul of Nature
The hidden soul of countless trees,
Of stones and flowers, wind and seas;
The spirit which urges birds to fly;
The secret way that flowers die;
The heart of every brook that leaps;
And every man when he finally sleeps.
(K.W., Santa Sabena Convent,
Sydney, Australia)

"Freeze A Moment"

Artists in many disciplines try to capture
moments that are memorable to them by
means of the tools of their art. The sculptor
uses marble; the musician, notes; the painter,
oils; and the photographer, film. The writer
has only words – often inadequate tools when
it comes to transmitting experiences that are
alive to him.

Ask the pupils to recall some moment they
remember vividly and to try to "freeze" it in
words, using only two lines. They may choose
a moment of movement (see the examples on
lightning, chapter 4, page 96), or an emotion
or a straight description. Whatever they
choose, their chief aim should be to catch the
instant as they experienced it, and make of it
a type of verbal slide. Although this is a difficult exercise, the discipline of attempting it
should help to make the young writers more
conscious of happenings around them.

Pond*
In a crystal looking-glass pond–
Plunk.

(P.H., Philaemon Wright High School, Hull, Canada)

Flame
A tongue of fire, a puff of wind,
A spiral of smoke, and all is still.

(V.M., Lyndon Institute, Lyndonville, U.S.A.)

---

* This piece can be used to trigger some interesting discussion on
the magnitude of the "plunk". What has fallen into the pond–a
raindrop, a frog, a piece of rock? If it is a piece of rock, how
big is it–a boulder, stone, pebble? Pupils should consider here the
element of *discrimination* in word choice; the fact that our
language contains sensitive words suitable for making fine
distinctions.

Sea Gull
Sea gull gliding on waves of air,
Sideways slipping, swooping–free.
(T.M., Foremark School, Derbyshire, England)

Father's Approval
A look of anger flashed across his face–
And then ne smiled.
(H.S., Outremont High School, Montreal, Canada)

Wave
It lived in green;
And died in white.
(J.P., Friends School, Hobart, Australia)

"I Like" Model

Ask the pupils to put together a poem with
a number of lines, each beginning with the
words "I like". This should be their own
piece, an expression of their personalities, a
statement of some of the things they like
best. If they know each other well, members
of a class might enjoy guessing who has done
each piece after the writing is completed.
Here are a few examples:

I like tandem bikes and pillow fighting:
I like blowing up ant holes with penny bangers,
    and eating Chinese food:
I like diving through the breakers at the beach,
    and the sound of traffic bustling in the city:
I like racing slot cars, and eating Kentucky fried
    chicken with my hands:
I like catching snakes and lizards, and trying
    things I've never done before:
I like excitement:
I like a lot.
(T.B., Coogee South School, Sydney, Australia)

I like to sit on the back of my chair:
I like the house I live in:
I like the joy of exam success,
    and to be by myself to think:
I like to go by the seashore
    and sit on pieces of driftwood:
I like exploring deep caves.

(A.W., Repton School, Derbyshire, England)

I like to look at things under my microscope:
I like to eat to my heart's content–
    Pizza with mushrooms and all that stuff:
I like to make things I haven't done before:
I like to read a lot–especially mysteries:
I like to breed fish:
I like so many things this paper can't say them all.

(J.R., St. Ignatius Loyola School, Montreal, Canada)

I like symphony orchestras,
    and bands with big beat;
I like the smell of new leather,
    and dark chilly nights;
I like the snow that falls on Christmas eve,
    and the bright lights in city shops;
I like roaring fires,
    and coming home to a hot meal after rain;
I like friendship.

(J.R., Henley Grammar School, Henley, England)

J'aime faire du ski sur les pentes enneigées;
J'aime me promener dans les champs,
    et ramasser de belles fleurs;
J'aime écouter le chant des oiseaux;
J'aime regarder nager les poissons dans l'eau claire;
J'aime mon chien et mon village.*

(S.D., École Primaire de Val d'Isère,
Savoie, France)

* translation - I like to ski on snow-covered slopes;
        I like to walk in the fields, and pick flowers;
        I like hearing the songs of birds;
        I like to watch fish swimming in clear water;
        I like my dog and my town.

Weather As Content

The weather has always interested writers both young and old. No matter where one lives, the weather takes many forms: wind, fog, rain, sun, cloud, heat, frost. It also has many moods, ranging from the benign to the tempestuous. Our own feelings and moods can be strongly conditioned by the weather. Ask the pupils to think about some condition of the weather they remember vividly, and to write a short piece about that moment. They should concentrate on portraying their own mood at the time, as well as the mood of the weather itself.

Sunshine

From behind a cloud
The sun appears,
Warming the cold ground
And the hearts of the people standing there;
Drying the raindrops on the long grass,
And the tears in the eyes of the children.

(A.B., Montreal West High School, Montreal, Canada)

Wind

The wind tears my jacket from my body;
The chill robs me of warmth;
I pass other cold, frozen faces on the paths
Without a word.

(M.H., Phillips Exeter Academy, Exeter, U.S.A.)

Snow

A heavy blanket,
Swirling,
Drifting,
Whirling,
Turning the world into a white heaven.

(P.H., Dorval High School, Montreal, Canada)

Rain
Walking at midnight through a field of grass,
Cold hard rain hitting my head
    and dripping down my neck;
A growl of thunder and a shaft
    of lightning,
Ripping the black from the
    sky for a moment,
Before it sends a shiver down my spine.

(M.S., Putney School, Putney, U.S.A.)

Sunset
Over the blue canvas it falls;
The paint gathers at the edge
Fiery gold and red;
The sun sinks through the
    clutches of the dark pines;
I like the twilight.

(B.C., Métis Beach School, Quebec, Canada)

Blizzard
Howling wind,
Huge mounds of snow,
Freezing.

Buried cars,
Frozen fingers,
Misery.

Driving gusts,
White-out snow,
Blinding.

(P.M., Hull Elementary School, Hull, Canada)

Using Mime

Most young people are highly physical. They are conscious of their limbs, of movement in general, and they enjoy games and strenuous activity. Teachers should capitalize on this physical resource by introducing their pupils to the art of mime. In doing so, it is important to stress at least two points. First, pupils should realize that when they mime – if only a

short thirty-second piece – they are not trying
to act, but to *live* a slice of life. They must
try not to be conscious of an audience, but
to concentrate on making what they are doing
as realistic as possible. Second, they should
be aware of pace and timing. Beginners
generally tend to rush their pieces, to present
them at an unnatural speed.

Ask the pupils to think up some simple sequence
of actions to present to the class. They needn't
have more than a minute or so to prepare. Some
of the following suggestions may serve as a
start, and many others can grow from them:

Driving a car
Getting out of bed in the morning
Raking leaves in the garden
Blowing up a balloon
Tying a tie in front of the mirror
Lighting a cigarette
Riding a horse
Sitting in the dentist's chair
Combing your hair
Playing tennis
Undoing a shoelace
Brushing your teeth
Rowing a boat.

Once the pupils have tried a solo item, let
them do pieces in teams of two or more. This
is a more difficult exercise, as it introduces
the element of co-ordination. Items such as
performing an operation, having a fight,
pulling in a tug-of-war, or playing instruments
in an orchestra are suitable for group mime.

After the pupils have seen fifteen or twenty
short pieces performed, ask them to write
about any aspect of the presentations that has
appealed to them. They need not describe

directly what they have seen. Their writing
may be about anything that the mime has
suggested to them. You may find that the
association of mime and written expression
stimulates a wide range of creative activities.

Personal Experience As Content

Young people generally express themselves
more easily and with greater impact if they
pick subjects from their own experience. Ask
them to write about anything that has actually
happened to them and to make their experience come alive by referring to the specific
details they remember. Obviously the range
of possible experiences here is almost limitless.
The important thing is that they be individual
and direct.

Climbing Mt. Wellington*
Run, walk, crawl, just get there;
Climb, climb, climb to the top;
Stretch out your hands, and pull yourself up;
Run, walk, crawl, just get there.
(J.A., Hutchins School, Hobart, Australia)

Running
My lungs move–burning;
My legs plod–heavily,
But the sweat feels refreshing.
(T.L., Phillips Exeter Academy, Exeter, U.S.A.)

Accident
It's hot,
But the wind in my face is cool
As I cruise along the road:
A quick look to the rear wheel

* The writer of this poem had just climbed Mt. Wellington which
  stands 4,000 feet above the city of Hobart, in Tasmania. A number
  of other members of his class, who had also completed the adventure, wrote with equal impact.

The shock–
The realization–
In slow motion the crunch
The jolt that knocks the wind out of me–
On my back on the hot road,
The clear sky above.

(J.Q., University of Toronto School, Toronto, Canada)

Une Avalanche*

Je jouais quand, tout a coup
J'entendis un grand bruit qui venait de la montagne;
Vite je me précipitai pour voir ce qui se passait:
Oh, une avalanche de la neige voltigeait par dessus
     des rochers;
De gros nuages blancs se formaient et s'échappaient;
Quel spectacle extraordinaire.

(P.C., École Primaire de Val d'Isère,
Savoie, France)

Oasis
Dust in my mouth and nose,
Hot dry air on my eyes;
A copper haze on the cliffs;
I come upon waterfalls–
Water slushing over heavy green moss–
Relief.

(P.H., Phillips Exeter Academy, Exeter, U.S.A.)

Physical Feelings

How frequently when asked the question,
"How are you feeling?", do we give an indef-

---

* The writer of this poem witnessed the tragic avalanche that took
  over 40 lives in his town in 1970.

  translation - I was playing when suddenly
                 I heard a roar coming from the mountain:
                 I hurried quickly to see what was happening:
                 An avalanche of snow was leaping over the rocks;
                 Huge white clouds were forming and billowing:
                 It was a horrifying spectacle.

inite answer such as "Fine," or "Not too bad,
thanks"? Such answers don't come to grips
with the question. You should encourage your
pupils to become conscious of their physical
feelings and to be specific in trying to record
them. Ask young writers to remember a
moment when physical feelings were dominant
– feelings of being out of breath, or having
frozen toes, or being "dog tired" – and to try
to make the moment come alive in words. The
main emphasis should be on detailing exactly
how they felt at the time. This exercise is far
from easy. Attempting it, however, should
add to the quality of living of each pupil.

Drowning*
No air;
Can't breathe;
Gasping;
Reaching out;
Gagging;
Lungs bursting;
Convulsions–
Air at last.

(B.H., Westmount High School,
Montreal, Canada)

My Motorbike
My bike is fast against the wind:
My life is free against the world;
I can feel the power beneath me,
The handle bars above;
The noise is silence to my ears;
My thoughts fly down the road.

(G.M., Central High School,
Moose Jaw, Canada)

Cross-Country Ski-Racing
Breathless and panting,
Breathing so hard–

---

* This poem was written by a pupil who nearly drowned in a canoe
accident.

Bend over and look at your toes;
Feel your legs heavy;
Thrust out your arms;
Feel the tug in your chest;
Breathless and panting,
Breathing so hard.

(T.V., Putney School, Putney, U.S.A.)

Faint
An eerie feeling of dopiness:
A loud buzzing in my ears:
A blurring of my sight,
Sudden nausea–
Faint.

(J.M., Brisbane Grammar School,
Brisbane, Australia)

Being Something Else

Ask the pupils to imagine that they are something else – an animal, insect, bird, or anything
that catches their imagination.* They must
"get inside" whatever they are thinking about
– into its heart and its head – and try to *be* that
thing. They must also imagine that, as that
thing, they can talk. What will they ask
for? complain about? be grateful for? This is
an exercise in empathy, in trying to understand
other things. They might start their written
piece by addressing some super-human being
such as "Great Spirit" or "Lord". However,
if using this approach, you should make it
clear that the poem is not meant to be
religious. The range of possible subjects here
is almost limitless. Some pupils might also
enjoy illustrating their pieces, as well.

---

* In her book *Prayers from the Ark* the French nun Carmen de
  Gatszold pursues a similar idea, but for animals and insects only.

Butterfly
Great Spirit,
I thank you for giving me freedom
From being a worm.
(I.G., Outremont High School, Montreal, Canada)

Desk
Lord,
People scratch their initials on me
So that other people may remember them:
Will anybody remember me?
(W.R., Phillips Academy, Andover, U.S.A.)

The
Great Spirit,
I am a word:
People call me 'the':
They use me so often that
        they lose my meaning;
I'm just a word to them—
Nothing more;
I know it's hard,
But help them to understand me.
(B.R., Punahou School, Honolulu, Hawaii)

Bee
Lord,
I'm a bee:
I'd rather be a tree,
And see the sea—
But trees are cut to make a house:
Lord,
I'd rather be a mouse,
And crawl and crawl,
And crawl about the house
And eat and run—
It would be fun
But O, what of the cat?
Lord,
I'd rather be the sun
And dance the sky—
I'd love to fly so high,
It would be fun to be the sun—

But Lord,
I guess I'd rather be a bee,
Because it's me
To be a bee.

(J.H., Riverview College, Sydney, Australia)

Inter-Office Memo
Great Spirit,
I'm an inter-office memo:
Please save me from the trash can.

(J.S., Punahou School, Honolulu, Hawaii)

Grass
Lord,
I'm a blade of grass:
People walk on me like I didn't exist:
Some guy cuts me with a mower,
And throws me on a pile to rot:
But Lord,
I guess that's what happens to everyone
In the end–
Just left to rot.

(H.M., St. George's School,
Vancouver, Canada)

Elephant
Great Spirit,
It's me–the elephant:
This is urgent:
Could you do something
About these mice?

(C.D., Hull Elementary School,
Hull, Canada)

Calf
Lord,
This is the calf, the new calf,
The one with the life sentence on his back:
If you're really watching over me,
Would you just drop in and open that wooden gate,
The one between me and the green grass
        and yellow dandelions.

(O.Z., Putney School, Putney, U.S.A.)

Using A Happening

The daily news is a constant source of material for writing. Whether it is an international event such as an earthquake or a space trip, a national happening such as a prime minister getting married, or a strictly local item such as the school team winning a big game–the news is always changing and often interesting. Ask the pupils to write about a current event that has particularly struck them. It need not be anything earth-shaking in significance. In fact, the more personal it is, the better. Remind them not to forget the humorous or the seemingly negative events. Often life's so-called "low moments" produce experiences of the greatest consequence.

Here too, the range of possible selections is wide, so one or two examples will suffice.

Blizzard*
The snow falls fast;
The shovels are busy;
I warm my hands,
And think of the summer:
I dream of the sun:
I think of warm air:
I imagine the water:
I feel its soft flow–
While mother yells at me:
"Keep shovelling."

(M.G., Wagar High School,
Montreal, Canada)

* This poem was written on the day of the most severe blizzard to hit
  Montreal in over twenty years.

The Grand Final*
It's seventy, sixty-eight–
To them:
Jezza marks
O what a gem–
His kick–
It's through for six.

(B.D., Sydney Grammar School,
Sydney, Australia)

Personal Reaction To A Topic

In an earlier exercise "Choosing a topic",
chapter 3, page 33, pupils were given a list of
suggested topics, and asked to pick one and
write about it in four lines or less. Most pupils
would probably have written about their
subject objectively; that is, they would have
given largely sensory descriptions, without
bringing their own feelings into the piece. Now
you might ask your pupils to go one step further,
and write about a topic of their own choice,
this time including their personal reaction to it,
or feeling about it. This exercise will add
other dimensions to their writing, of involvement, mood, subjectivity.

As in the earlier exercise, pupils will benefit
from some suggestions from you. These suggestions should offer scope for interpretation,
and in this sense should be less concrete than the
earlier ones. Again, you should try to develop
an ever-growing list of suggestions, calling on
the pupils themselves for help in compiling it.

* This poem was written by a boy who had just watched the 1970
Grand Final in Australian Rules Football – a classic contest.

Here are a few lists—arranged in groups of five*
items—as a starter:

I	II
The sky at night	Midday in the bush
Bargain counter at rush hour	Traffic jam
The summit	Sprained ankle
Roast dinner	Discotheque
Shearing	Walls

III	IV
Storm at sea	Frosted pane
Colors on an oily puddle	Farewells
Screeching tires	Burning fever
Footprints in sand	Speed
The opening kickoff	Bleeding nose

V	VI
Sandpaper	The last fifty yards
First kiss	Flashing neon lights
Eyes	Siren
Pop concert	Shadows
Ant hill	Seeds

After the pupil has made his choice, he should
write about his topic in five lines or less, again
concentrating on conciseness and economy of
expression.

Speed
The feel of wind rushing past my face
Excites me;
I like doing long fast turns
On my bicycle:
I love doing skids on wet grass.
(M.C., Sydney Grammar School, Sydney, Australia)

---

* The smaller number is advisable here because of the added dimension of the exercise.

Disco
Singing, dancing to let out my feeling,
Loud, living music to which you can move;
Teenagers everywhere, seldom appealing
To out-dated oldies who can't get in the groove.
(W.T., Brisbane Grammar School, Brisbane, Australia)

Speed
A sensational feeling–
The next best thing to watching TV:
Fun if you're wearing a seat belt:
I like it.
(R.C., St. Johnsbury Academy, St. Johnsbury, U.S.A.)

Walls
Walls are for posters of Hendrix and Surf:
For keeping warm, and keeping cool;
Walls are great.
(P.L.G., The King's School, Parramatta, Australia)

Pop Concert
Manfred Man does his thing:
He announces joy
With his junk:
He turns us on:
His beat is gas.
(D.P., Verdun High School, Montreal, Canada)

Animal Songs

Young people in every country appear to have
a liking for and empathy with animals.
Whether household pets, zoo animals, or even
animals in photographs, all hold a
fascination for the young. You might try to
capitalize on this interest for a writing exercise.
Ask your pupils to describe the animal of their
choice as if from the inside. They should try
to capture its personality, and outstanding
characteristics, and habits. This exercise
should help them to realize that animals have
an individuality, much as humans do. An
understanding of personality is based, in part,
on close observation.

Leopard
Gentle hunter
His tail plays on the ground
While he crushes the skull.

Beautiful death
Who puts on a spotted robe
When he goes to his victim.

Playful killer
Whose loving embrace
Splits the antelope's heart.*

Cat
She moves quietly–
At her pace
Content to be alone–
Still and suspicious.
She sleeps all day:
At night
The house is her jungle.

(D.B., Dunton High School, Montreal, Canada)

Snail
All the time that ever was,
To reach a tree he cannot see,
To climb a wall he'll never reach,
To eat a leaf he'll never find.
All the time there'll ever be,
To climb a brick, or move a stick;
To eat, and sleep, and crawl, and drink;
All the time in the world to think.

(S.A., Repton School, Derbyshire, England)

Rhino
His charge is swift and straight,
But usually fails to find the target:
His eyes mean, weak, and small;
His hide like a cemented wall;
His brain really crawls–
But his temper makes up for that.

(D.G., St. Paul's School, Darjeeling, India)

* This poem, quoted from *Ijala* (Papuan Pocket Poets, Editor Uli Beier) is by a young pupil who obviously knew the habits of his subject.

Goldfish
Wide-eyed
With flapping fins,
Its body curves and swerves;
Its slimy feel slowly slides
Across the glass bowl,
Slowly–
Always in circles.

(C.B., Wagar High School, Montreal, Canada)

Hedgehog
The hedgehog–
Spined scrounger,
Peers from his nest,
And sets out to find some messy meal:
His small face under black spines
Peers into heavy bush:
Danger may lurk there.

(B.E., Bilton Grange School, Dunchurch, England)

Monkeys
Monkeys jump from tree to tree
To get a punch at one another,
To fight their heads off,
To bully the weak ones.
Monkeys go to sleep early,
To get up early,
To chatter the earliest,
To awaken the jungle,
To go ahead with their pranks,
All through the day.

(A.D., Jamhuri High School, Nairobi, Kenya)

Advertisement

We live in a world of mass communication
where multi-media presentations influence our
daily thinking and action. Young people are
conscious of television, the radio, signboards,
and many other forms of advertising. Ask
your pupils to become Madison Avenue copy-
writers for a day. First they are to invent a

product (it must not be anything with a
recognized brand) and give it a name. Then
they are to write a five-line advertisement for
it, convincing prospective buyers of its merits
and distinctive features. The first and last
lines of their advertisement simply name the
product. The middle three lines extol its
virtues. Encourage them to be imaginative,
and to use any of the devices they have
noticed in commercial advertisements.* The
results should prove interesting, perhaps even
saleable.

Smog's Toffees
Smog's toffees,
Stretchy, gooey, sticky,
Pulls at your teeth, clings to your jaw
Smooth–
Smog's toffees.
(P.C., Coogee South School, Sydney, Australia)

Gaspo Plasto
Gaspo plasto–
Its gooey feel,
It's dripping and slips like soap,
It's pink and soft–I want to eat it;
Gaspo plasto.
(P.M., Punahou School, Honolulu, Hawaii)

Dirt
Dirt,
Good to play in;
Grows things;
Plenty of it;
Dirt.
(I.L., Westbrook School, Montreal, Canada)

---

* Here the opportunity arises for a discussion of the techniques used
and deceptions employed in everyday advertisements. Pupils might
bring specific examples to class for analysis.

Wigs
Wigs,
Very hairy,
Fit all sizes,
Round heads, square heads, fat heads
Wigs.
(P.R., Friends School, Hobart, Australia)

Being Alive

Recently I discovered a book entitled *To Be Alive*. It was a book largely composed of pictures showing people of various ages engaged in activities which they really enjoyed. At the moments shown, these people were evidently living, as opposed to merely existing.

Ask the pupils to think of moments when, for them, life is full. Any experience will do–eating, hobbies, sport, thinking–any involvement that gives them pleasure. They should combine these moments and experiences into a piece of writing of about six to ten lines in length, which they might call "Being Alive". The well-written piece should serve as a type of portrait of the individual who has made it. Here are a few examples, with the ages of the writers attached:

Being alive is eating an egg-roll bought with your
     last 20¢;
Walking in puddles with your best shoes on;
Getting in trouble on the first day of school–
That's being alive.
Having a fight and then making up;
Running downhill unable to stop–
Feeling as if you could fly;
Hearing the surf crash on the shore,
Smelling the cinnamon in rich apple pie–
That's being alive.
(S.D., age 14, Marymount High School, Montreal, Canada)

Going ski-dooing,
Or maybe skiing,
Throwing a snowball,
That's being alive:
Making go-karts,
Or building forts,
Driving a bike,
That's being alive:
Going places,
Fooling around,
Doing arithmetic,
That's being alive.

(R.T., age 10, Gatineau Mills Elementary School,
Quebec, Canada)

Two different kinds of ice cream,
Tieing your shoe for the first time,
Knowing a secret,
Telling the time–
That's being alive:
Being alone every now and then;
Banging your drum in your room;
Having a dachshund puppy–
That's being alive.

(K.L., age 12, Otter Valley High School, Brandon, U.S.A.)

After each pupil in the class has written his
piece, you might collect the work and read a
number aloud, asking the pupils to guess who
has written each one.

Mood of A Season

Ask each pupil to pick one of the four seasons,
and to write a short piece in which he tries to
capture the mood of his season. This is no
easy task. Perhaps, as a start, he might
benefit from writing down a number of adjectives which are appropriate to each season.
For example:

SPRING: bright, clean, born again, singing, joy-

SUMMER:
> ful, yellow, lion-hearted, colourful, dew-touched, breezy.

SUMMER:
> lazy, pleasant, golden, sleepy, green, unruffled, shimmering, lethargic, buzzing, sweating

AUTUMN:
> rusty, fickle, changeable, capricious, wind-blown, exciting, decaying, mellow-mild

WINTER:
> harsh, vindictive, cruel, angry, bitter, relentless, uncompromising, unfriendly, gloomy, depressing, dark, icy

The appropriateness of these adjectives will depend, of course, on the country – or part of the country – to which they refer. Winter in the far north of Canada is a very different season from winter in Queensland, Australia, for instance. Once the pupils have put down their adjectives, ask them to write a piece of six lines or less in which they try to portray the mood of their season.

Autumn
The sun shines through the air and thinning trees;
It reflects off sunken leaves in the lazy stream
In dazzling patterns that light the dark bank.
(D.O., John Grant High School, Montreal, Canada)

Winter
Somewnere the dirt-grey snow
   and cloud-grey sky meet:
There is nothing else
Except the black, unmoving tree.
(P.K., Dunton High School, Montreal, Canada)

Autumn
The trees are raked by the blowing wind:
The sky is filled with red and orange;
My spirit flies.
(J.F., Phillips Exeter Academy, Exeter, U.S.A.)

Winter
Withered vine;
Rotten tree;
Dark crow;
Lean horse;
Broken-hearted man in despair.
(M.C., Raffles Institution, Singapore)

Summer
The sky spreads blue and restful,
Metallic in its depth:
I lie here,
Sleepy, content,
Sharing its mood.
(T.V., Foremark School, Derbyshire, England)

Winter
Winter is cross,
Snaps at our feet
Like a dog on the loose.
(J.C., Repton School, Derbyshire, England)

Writing From A Picture

Every teacher should establish and develop a
collection of dramatic pictures for use in the
classroom. These you may gather from glossy
magazines, newspapers, photo-print shops or
any number of other sources. Interesting,
startling, or amusing examples should not be
hard to find. You might want to mount your
pictures on a cardboard background for easier
handling and display.

Let the pupils look at a range of pictures,
each chosen for some distinct feature, and
then write a piece about anything that one
of the pictures suggests to them. Here are
two pieces written by two different boys. They

had just been shown a picture of a man
kneeling in the mud beside a giant transport
truck with a flat tire. The punctured tire is, in
reality, at least eight feet in diameter. As the
man surveys it he has a look of hopelessness
on his face, and his arms are spread wide in a
"what-do-I-do-now?" gesture.

Tire
Big, bulky, black,
Round and round,
Splashing through puddles—
Raising the dust;
After fifty thousand miles,
It is ready to bust.
Why here?
(A.S., St. George's School, Montreal, Canada)

Massive,
Round,
Eight feet high;
If another one blows,
I'll just about die.
(C.D., St. George's School, Montreal, Canada)

Various kinds of pictures are suitable for this
exercise; for example, detailed close-ups of
flowers or animals; action shots of sports;
wide-angled views of landscapes or the
surface of the moon; expressions on people's
faces; candid-camera exposés of life's humorous moments; and many more. Encourage
the pupils to find their own pictures and
bring them to class to enjoy with the others.
Discovering appropriate pictures is a lesson in
itself, and demands a discipline closely related
to the skill involved in isolating a subject
about which to write.

Invent A "Something"

Most young people have active imaginations, particularly if they are allowed to pretend or make things up. In this exercise, ask each of them to invent something. It might be an animal, object, person, or a purely imaginary creature. Have them give it a name, and then write about it. They should tell what it looks like, what it wears, what it eats, what it does for a living – in fact, any details that will make it realistic for the reader. Encourage them to be adventurous in their creations. Their "somethings" need not – in fact, probably should not – actually exist. Some of the pupils might get enjoyment from illustrating their writing.

Here are a few examples to help you begin:

The Serre
He has a round beaming face
    and a friendly smile –
A soft pot belly,
    and floppy legs.
His eyes gleam green
    phosphoresence in the dark –
And he's mine.
(B.R., Montreal West High School, Montreal, Canada)

Treakle Wit (A Chalk Tiger)
I am on the blackboard;
My face is like the face of the sun;
I am just about to jump down;
It is like running through tunnels isn't it?
I am going to explore the classrooms;
Come with me, come on.
(B.D., Foremark School, Derbyshire, England)

Treakle Wit*

He's gone, poor Treakle Wit;
Made in our lesson, gone in our lesson;
Destroyed, wiped off the face of the earth;
He had a sweet smile, a full moon face;
He held up a helpless paw;
He can't climb out now;
He's gone.

(A.S., Foremark School, Derbyshire, England)

Laughabug

The laughabug appears in strange places:
It lies in a lump amongst
    strings, marbles, and frogs in boys' pockets;
It creeps into socks and sweaters,
    and tickles the skin;
It fits into shoe eyelets, and
    nibbles at laces:
Beware:
The laughabug is after you.

(C.F., Canberra Grammar School, Canberra, Australia)

---

* This poem, written by another boy in the same class is a sequel to
the one above. Perhaps its young writer did not realize that once
something has impressed itself on the mind, it never disappears
entirely.

The Meco Man
This man is mechanical,
Square in appearance;
With coal black eyes—
Never a smile has he:
Nuts, bolts, and wires make up his insides:
'Yes',
'No',
All his thoughts are concise:
Cold and unfeeling,
The Meco man has no heart.

(P.D., Newton High School, Boston, U.S.A.)

Here are some other creatures that have been invented by pupils. You will probably find many ingenious and amusing examples in the work of your own pupils.

groofs—they hide in fog, and make you feel
     creepy.
twarfs—they live in the woodwork shop, and
     mess up your carpentry.
skgwiffs—they exist in the soles of shoes, and
     make them squeak.
doodlebugs—they grow in exercise books during
     boring classes.

Humorous Moment

Everyone enjoys a laugh. Particularly in moments of tension or crisis it is important to retain a sense of humour and not get too serious about things. Ask the pupils to recall some moment that, for them, had a humorous aspect to it. This moment might be an actual event, or simply a thought or a reaction to some happening. They should try to bring out the humour of the moment in their writing. A word here about not forcing humour would be appropriate. Beginners sometimes try too hard to be funny unless they are warned against this tendency. Humour has many faces, as the examples below indicate.

Rugby Forward (with apologies to Blake)
Forward, forward feeling numb,
In the jungles of the scrum;
What immortal curse or threat
Makes you shove, and grunt, and sweat?

Forward, forward in the muck,
At the bottom of the ruck:
You jump, and run, and fall, and try–
Do you really want to die?

(D.W., Brisbane Grammar School, Brisbane, Australia)

Electioneers
'Give me your vote–
I'll mend your roads and bridges
Raise your wages:'
These talks make funny talkers;
Electioneers all act like jokers.

(A.T., St. Paul's School, Darjeeling, India)

Dish Washing
My big brother washes;
My big sister dries;
My mother puts away;
I watch T.V.

(C.W., Friends School, Hobart, Australia)

Pale-Face Visit*
The classroom is silent, filled with pupils
Doing their work unsmilingly;
Suddenly the silence is broken by welcome news:
A dignified pale-faced teacher is coming:
We are happy;
What is a pale-face doing in a place like this?
Answer–
At last the pale-face has found civilization.

(M.W., Raffles Institution, Singapore)

* The 'pale-face' referred to is the author on the occasion of his visit to this largely Asian-Indian school.

Honey
When all that honey went
    all over Charlie's pyjamas—
What a waste of honey.

(R.P., Downlands College, Toowoomba, Australia)

Describing Your Own Country, City, Or Town

Most people have pride in their own country
and in the particular place where they live.
This pride stems partly, perhaps, from familiar-
ity. We often like best what we know best.
You might use this fact to initiate a writing
exercise. Ask the pupils to write a short piece
describing their own country, city, or town.
Tell them not to mention directly the place
they are writing about anywhere other than in
the title. Rather they must try to give the outstanding characteristics and features of their
area, so that anyone familiar with it may be
able to guess the location. This exercise might
also serve as a stimulus to local environment
studies, or be used as an exchange of infor-
mation between "pen-pal" associates.

Here are several pieces written in various parts
of the world. The title is located below each
poem. See if the pupils can guess them.

Sunshine burning down;
No fumes to strangle the air;
Wide open spaces,
Time to go places;
Great national parks,
Or underwater beauty.

(J.H., Brisbane Grammar School, Brisbane, Australia)
title: Queensland, Australia

A sweet, sour smell of the river;
A walk across the bridge;
A narrow stifling alley:
Bags, slippers –
Money moves from hand to hand;
Instant Asia.

(H.H., Raffles Institution, Singapore)
title: Singapore

Sunshine tanning your skin:
Beaches on which to swim:
Cold mountains to climb,
Animals to enjoy;
Everywhere the spirit of harambee.

(P.S., Jamhuri High School, Nairobi, Kenya)
title: Kenya

The horn of Africa,
Thirteen months of sunshine;
Famous for honoring visitors –
High and clear,
An island of Christianity;
A basket of bread.

(C.E., Commercial High School, Addis Ababa, Ethiopia)
title: Ethiopia

Mirages quiver;
Sun beams blind;
Sandy soil burns bare feet;
The hot wind evaporates sweat.

(T.H., Marine Military Academy, Harlingen, U.S.A.)
title: Texas

The fish stink;
Ships come to and fro,
Loaded with Carlsberg beer:
Docks are scattered around:
Rainbows are on the water as oil floats by.

(P.H., St. Edmund's School, Canterbury, England)
title: Goole, Yorkshire (England)

Sweet smelling hops,
Clouds hurrying across the sky;
Oast houses scattered around the land;
Rain falling silently.

(P.D., King's School, Canterbury, England)
title: Kent (England)

Motor-powered rickshaws,
Camels in the streets;
Parched scrub-land all around;
Mosquitoes,
Houses squashed in;
People jammed.

(C.H., Foremark School, Derbyshire, England)
title: Karachi (Pakistan)

Crowded and noisy,
Petrol fumes,
Tycoons in Rolls Royces,
Houses covered with pigeons;
A tourist attraction for miles around.

(S.B., Repton School, Derbyshire, England)
title: London

A small village on the A5 Road,
The clock tower stands
Outside the railway station
Which boasts
The longest platform tickets in Europe.

(A.S., Repton School, Derbyshire, England)
title: Llanfairpwllgwyngyllgoger—
       ichwryndrobwllillantisiliogogogoch. *

A Sense Of Wonder

Young people, particularly the very young,
are usually filled with a sense of wonder. They
show awe and amazement in the things around
them; what the French call *émerveillement*.
They are filled with questions. (Why is the
grass green? Why doesn't that plane up there
fall into the ground? How do geese know when
it's time to fly south?) As we grow older, we

* A small village on the island of Anglesey,
  Wales. Its name was originally shorter, but an
  eccentric curate made up the present one.
  Platform tickets are on sale at the railway
  station for 5¢ and are 5 inches long.

are in danger of losing this sense of wonder, this delight in simple things.

Ask the pupils to think back to a time when they experienced this sense of amazement. It might have been at daybreak on a lake as the first rays of the sun turned the water to gold; or on a crowded city street at rush hour; or in the silence of thought. Whatever the situation, they should try to make their feelings of the moment come alive in ten lines or fewer.

It is always difficult to give life to experiences when all we have to work with is words. Nonetheless, the attempt itself is worthwhile, particularly when we are recalling rich moments. Here are the efforts of several young people at re-creating their own particular sense of wonder.

Christmas*
Coming into the room
I see the decorated tree:
My eyes start to look around:
Dad says: "Look around"
There they are–snowshoes.
(B.W., Brandon Graded School, Brandon, U.S.A.)

Spray
You feel the tingles on your face–
Again,
and again,
and again,
Until you turn away to brace
The wonder of where it comes from.
(R.M., St. John's School, Selkirk, Canada)

---

* In this particular part of rural Vermont, boys are given snowshoes only at age eight or nine, when parents feel that they are responsible enough to explore the woods and mountains alone. Hence snowshoes are a possession fondly desired by most Vermont young people as their keys to adventure and independence.

L'Edelweiss*

On ceuille l'edelweiss dans les endroits rocheux;
Elle est blanche, avec de petites feuilles grisâtres;
Autour d'elle de petits cailloux scintillent au soleil;
Quel plaisir d'aller la ramasser dans les montagnes
    ensoleillées.

(D.C., École Primaire de Val d'Isère, Savoie, France)

Words

There is a man who will show you
The life in words:
On winter days you may find him perched
In the door of his igloo;
And as his face of shiny leather moves,
You may begin, if you try, to let your own words
Come out to play together in the blinding winter sun:
You will never understand his lesson
If you lean too much on meaning;
It will be your heart
That will make your head feel larger.

(W.S., Phillips Exeter Academy, Exeter, U.S.A.)

People

People–
Extending a helping hand,
Exchanging a smile,
The sound of laughter in the air,
Together, sharing each other.

(P.M., Punahou School, Honolulu, Hawaii)

Canoe Trip

I walk down the trail
My pack on my back–
Wilderness and quiet about.

(T.S., St. George's School, Vancouver, Canada)

---

* translation– The Edelweiss (An Alpine flower)
           We pick the edelweiss in rocky places;
           It is a white flower with greyish petals;
           Around it, small pebbles glitter in the sunlight;
           What fun it is to gather the edelweiss
           On sun-drenched mountain sides.

Cat
At the first warm sunshine
Our cat dances
Black on green grass,
Bringing summer happiness out.
(M.P., Central High School, Moose Jaw, Canada)

Magpie
Scavenging, pecking,
Waddling slowly,
Investigating proudly,
Tail turned up,
Silhouetted in black and white–
Nature's wonder.
(M.W., The King's School, Parramatta, Australia)

What Really Excites You?

Most young people have a variety of interests about which they are enthusiastic. They may have little to do with school, but are no less important to their education. Ask each pupil to think about something that really excites him and to write a short piece about it. It can be anything–hobbies, eating, reading, music, collecting things, sport, recreation activities, travel–so long as it genuinely interests him. An aim of this exercise is to share his enthusiasm with others. He should try to make the subject seem meaningful and vital, even to those who know little about it. A pupil can frequently spark his enthusiasm for other things if he starts by concentrating on something in which he is particularly interested.

Football
I like the feeling
As my muscles tighten
And I can let off a little steam.
(G.D., Sydney Grammar School, Sydney, Australia)

A Chinese Dish
The day I tasted it
My heart was delighted;
It was a Chinese dish,
Of fried rice and prawns;
So appetising it was that,
Even today, thinking of it,
Makes my mouth watery.

(R.R., Garoka High School, Garoka, New Guinea)

Painting
Bristly brush–
Colored slush,
A bright red splash,
Comes down with a flash.

(A.D., Dunton High School, Montreal, Canada)

Sailing
Shooting snow-capped rollers,
Tumbling into troughs,
Racing with gulls,
Planing with the wind,
Swimming in the drink–
I couldn't think a bit,
Without thinking a bit about sailing.

(R.B., Sydney Grammar School, Sydney, Australia)

Grime
Summer grime,
Winter grime,
Sludgy, slimy all the time;
Gooey grime,
Grim grime,
Things are grimy all the time;
Smelly soot,
Looks like grime,
But different, different all the time:
Summer grime,
Winter grime,
Muggy, moody all the time:
Kids are clean,
Mothers mean,
Grime for all time.

(T.M., Crown Woods Comprehensive School, London, England)

Skating
Flying over ice –
Smooth ice –
Opaque.
Making figures,
Gliding –
Cool.
Spinning,
Jumping,
Wow.

(P.S., Westmount High School, Montreal, Canada)

Chapter 4   Evaluative
Criteria

Writing is a craft, and as such it involves certain specific skills. In order to achieve effective expression, pupils have to learn these skills and then try to practise them in their work. With writing, as with most other accomplishments, there is no easy road to success. Learning to write takes time and effort. This chapter outlines a number of skills that should be useful to the young writer in improving his expression. It should also provide him with some basic standards with which to evaluate his own writing.

Choice Of The Word

At the heart of all expression lies the task of picking the precise word for a given context. The beginner should concentrate on the individual word before he attempts more extensive verbal structures. This task requires discrimination. As an exercise, ask the pupils what verb they would use to describe the moon on a clear night. Discuss a number of possibilities; for example, gleams, shines, shimmers, radiates. Each verb conveys its own shade of meaning and some are more appropriate than others. The verb "glows", for instance, is probably inappropriate.because it implies heat, and even suggests the colours red and orange. A thesaurus is useful in developing this kind of discrimination.

In addition, discuss the literal meaning of words with your pupils. An cxamplc such as the one on "leopard" (chapter 3, page 63) is helpful in this context:

Playful killer
Whose loving embrace
Splits the antelope's heart.

Normally if we talk of "breaking someone's heart", we do not use the verb "break" in a literal sense. But the pupil who wrote about the leopard knew the habits of the animal and used, in this case, the verb "splits" literally. Make up other examples of a similar type, or have the pupils bring their own illustrations for class discussion.

The three-word model ending with an adverb (chapter 2, page 18) also offers the opportunity for word choice. Consider this example written by a distinguished Australian teacher of English whose wife had recently given birth:

> babies
> burp
> b _____ ly

What adverb would be most appropriate here? Obviously the choice hinges on the exact meaning the writer is trying to convey. There are many possibilities – bountifully, boldly, brazenly, brashly, beautifully, bashfully, blissfully – to name but a few. Let us examine each of these in turn:

bountifully	not entirely appropriate: its dictionary definition doesn't coincide with what the writer is trying to say.
boldly	a good choice: concise and to the point; accurate.
brazenly	a little strong perhaps; suggests intentional forcefulness which a baby probably doesn't have.
brashly	again the tone is rather strong; the baby probably means no harm.

beautifully	over-used word; only the mother would think so.
bashfully	a poor choice. It isn't true. Babies don't know enough to be bashful.
blissfully	not a bad choice. It would appear to be true.

This example illustrates some of the complexities involved in picking a word for a context. (The teacher picked the adverb "boldly" for his piece.) The process demands patience, thought, and the ability to discriminate. It is the starting point for all achievement in writing.

Structure

One of the elements that distinguishes poetry from prose is structure. Whereas prose usually appears in sentences and linked paragraphs, poetry can assume a variety of forms, depending on the aims of the writer. Pupils should be shown some of the options open to them in choosing the structure of their work. Consider the following first draft of a piece written by an Australian pupil who had just taken a trip across the barren Nullabor plain:

> Flat as far as the eye can see
> And no trees only scrub and
> Flat no trees no water no people
> No hills. No anything except desolation.

After producing this draft, the writer felt she wanted to change its structure. She felt she should remove "and" and "only" in the second line, and "no people" in the third. In the fourth, she wanted to contract "no anything" to "nothing", and eliminate the word "except".

But the most important alterations she made
on successive revisions of the piece concerned
its shape. Her final version looked like this:

Flat –
As far as the eye can see,
No trees:
Scrub and flat,
No trees:
No water;
No hills;
Nothing –
Desolation.

(G.B., Friends School, Hobart, Australia)

She retained one long line, the second, to give
the dominant impression of the flatness of the
plain. Otherwise, she grouped her lines for
effectiveness of rhythm. Thus her final version
sounds better when read aloud, and has a form
more appropriate to the subject about which
it is written.

Flexibility of structure affords the writer an
opportunity to give prominence to single
words or combinations of words. For example,
in this piece by a New Guinea boy, the word
"mosquitoes" occupies a single line in order to
achieve visual prominence:

Walking and running we entered the forest,
Our first enemy met us,
Mosquitoes.
From our heads to our feet,
In thousands they attacked us,
In thousands they came.

(L.G., Garoka Teachers' College, Garoka, New Guinea.)

By placing the word on a line by itself, the
writer arrests the eye of the reader, and hence

underscores the importance of "mosquitoes" in a way which would not be possible in prose.

Pupils should experiment with various optical patterns (see chapter 5, page 123), so that they are aware of the options available and their contribution to form. They should realize that experienced writers have a reason for the structures they select, and that forms is an integral part of the fabric of poetry.

Accuracy

Another characteristic of expression that young writers must recognize is accuracy. With beginners, in particular, the temptation exists to put things down simply because they sound good, or because they have a familiar ring to them. Any expression that is used in a piece should be correct and true to fact. Otherwise readers will be misled by mere verbal gymnastics.

Consider this example written in Vermont, U.S.A., and intended to portray a month of the year. (An exercise of this type is introduced in chapter 5 under the heading, "Portrait of a Month".) Read the piece, and then fill in the blank with the name of the month.

This winter's white on last year's green-
Sagging _____ snowman.

(B.P., Lyndon Institute, Lyndonville, U.S.A.)

The writer has titled his piece *November*. Uncertainty exists here, however, as to the interpretation of the phrase "last year's green." Does the writer mean the green of the last calendar year, or does he mean last season's green; i.e., the green of nature? His title suggests he means the latter.

Another useful exercise in accuracy of expression is provided by the ideogram model. (See chapter 5, page 108 for a full description of this model.) In this exercise the pupil writes a short piece which accurately describes the shape of any letter of the alphabet or any number of his choice. If his piece is descriptively accurate, then the reader should be able to guess the topic. For example, to what letter does the following model refer?

A camel who has just had a huge drink,
Lying on his back,
With his feet in the air.

(T.S., Crown Woods Comprehensive School, London, England)

The pupils should be able to guess the letter "w" from this word portrait.

This exercise can be extended to apply to Chinese or any other symbol language. Try to construct the symbol described in these words:

A table on top of a stone;
A box on top of the table;
A plate on top of the box;
A stick sticking into the plate.

(T.S., Raffles Institution, Singapore)

This piece, written in English by a Chinese pupil, is the symbol for "high".

or:

A spike through
A gaping mouth.

(M.R., Raffles Institution, Singapore)

These lines describe the Chinese symbol for "middle" or "centre." Without accuracy of expression, the guessing of both symbols would be difficult, if not impossible.

Honesty of Expression

An extension of the concept of accuracy involves honesty of expression. Young writers should be taught that a search for truth in their pieces is important. Art seeks to reveal truth as the artist sees it, to portray things with honesty and sincerity. Consider the following poem:

Fire Hydrant
Lord,
This is the fire hydrant;
Please save me from the dogs;
They'll drown me.
(C.S., Ross School, Moose Jaw, Canada)

This poem was written by a young boy after he had considered the fire hydrant standing in his school playground. The piece was not written for shock effect. The writer simply associated fire hydrants and dogs in his mind, and wrote about them. Pupils should be encouraged to express themselves honestly and without fear.

Rhythm

An element basic to all writing, whether prose or poetry, is rhythm. Here is what David McCord, one of the foremost contemporary American poets, has to say about it:

"One of the things I learned as a country boy on Long Island and out in Oregon was to see, hear, feel, and breathe the rhythm of the earth. This is another way of saying that I learned

very early something of the poetry of life. For
poetry, remember, is *not* rhyme or tricks with
words; or wit, laughter, grief, tears and nonsense, though all these things are, in their
way, part of written poetry. Poetry essentially
is rhythm, as life is rhythm. No one fails to
observe the rise and setting of the sun, the
endless rhythm of the journeying clouds; of
rivers, brooks, waves on the beach, leaves in
motion on a tree.

"We speak, sing, and act with rhythm. Most
physical games – tennis, for example – are highly
rhythmical; the good driver drives his car with
rhythm. And so the best writing, poetry or
prose – quite apart from meaning – depends on a
very sure and subtle control of its flow.

"Watch a poet. He is weighing the reaction
between lines, between words, between con-
sonants in harmony with vowels and the
specific order in which these reactions occur.

The tiger lily is a panther,
Orange to black spot;
Her tongue is the velvet pretty anther
And she's in the vacant lot.

"Note that I do not say pretty velvet anther
which is prose, but velvet pretty anther – a far
better and smoother arrangement of these
words."*

David McCord attributes his own sense of
rhythm to at least two influences. He learned
Morse code as a young man, and had an
operator's licence by the time he was sixteen.
In addition, his grandmother read aloud to him
the entire King James' version of the Bible.

* Extract taken from the record jacket to "The Pickety Fence and
  other Poems" by David McCord (Pathways of Sound, Inc.).

Much of it is written in a flowing English style on which we have not been able to improve in over three and a half centuries – and its rhythm has stuck for McCord. These two influences have established a feeling for rhythm in his mind which is apparent in his writing. Take his poem "The Pickety Fence", for example:

The pickety fence,
The pickety fence,
Give it a lick it's
The pickety fence:
Give it a lick it's
The clickety fence
Give it a lick it's
A lickety fence
Give it a lick
Give it a lick
Give it a lick
With a rickety stick
Pickety
Pickety
Pickety
Pick.

Formal Rhythm

Some pupils, perhaps because of earlier exposure to nursery rhymes, may want to experiment with verse that has set scansion. You should introduce them to the technical aspects of different poetic measures, and show them how to establish the beat in a line by marking the accented and unaccented syllables:

Ĭ WÁN   DEŘED LÓNE   LЎ ÁS Ă CLÓUD*

---

* This line, and subsequent ones in Wordsworth's "Daffodils", is in iambic tetrameter; i.e., four feet, each consisting of an unaccented syllable followed by an accented one.

Once they have some technical knowledge,
encourage them to write pieces of their own
in set metre. The ballad stanza is usually a
popular choice.

Rhythm in Writing

Poetry need not always make logical sense. In
fact, you should encourage your pupils to
write a piece for the simple purpose of creating
a sound effect. The writing may be nonsense
as far as reason is concerned, but it must have
a certain pattern in rhythm and sound. Here
are a few examples:

Raindrops
Pitter, patter falling hard,
Splishing, splashing dropping far;
Pitter, patter pounding down,
Splishing, splashing with a frown;
Pitter, splish,
Patter, splash,
In a puddle, down we crash.
(T.P., Dunton High School, Montreal, Canada)

Alley Cat
Clink,
Clank,
Clash,
Another one down—
Dirty old rubbish cans—
What have you found?
Fish bones?
Stale bread?
(C.S., Presbyterian Ladies College, Warwick, Australia)

American Mis-Education
Let us out;
Let us grow;
Let us listen;
Let us know;
Let us learn;

Let us do;
Let us be;
Let us go.

(J.W., Harvard Education School, Cambridge, U.S.A.)

Ivy

Ivy crashes in the fall,
Tumbling in rivers
                    down
                    the
                    wall:
The grass is blue;
The sky is green;
And all the leaves
Are left unseen.
Pastoral mumbles the meadow heath,
And the down wind up comes over neath;
Ivy crashes in the fall,
Tumbling in rivers
                    down
                    the
                    wall.

(P.O., Phillips Exeter Academy, Exeter, U.S.A.)

Pupils should learn to concentrate on the
rhythm of their writing. They should read
their work out loud, particularly in the early
stages of writing, so that they are aware of the
sound effects they are creating. Poetry, like
music, is meant to be heard.

Appropriateness

One of the criteria of judgment applicable to
the choice of any word or combination of
words is appropriateness. Is it the right word
for the context? Appropriateness is a quality
which includes a number of elements, among
them mood, intention, correctness, and rhythm.
As an exercise in appropriate word choice,

ask the pupils to "freeze" some moment that they remember vividly, using only two lines. Essentially they are attempting to do with their pen and words what a photographer does with his camera and film. They should think of some aspect of movement – a bird flying, a tree bending in the wind, a racing car driving around a curve on a track – and try to capture this movement in words.

Consider the following pieces done by two different young writers, but both about the same subject, lightning. Ask the pupils to determine which of the two is the more appropriate to the subject:

(1) The lightning flashed, a sheath of white,
      Its powerful outbreak awakened the night.

(J.F., Outremont High School, Montreal, Canada)

(2) The lightning came:
      It flashed, and went.

(V.C., Bishop's College School, Lennoxville, Canada)

A number of factors should be considered here. First, rhythm. If the pupils listen to the first piece carefully, they will hear a rhythm which almost scans. But does lightning strike with a set pattern and flow? Surely not. It is jagged, irregular. Hence the first piece may sound good, but this does not make it appropriate.

Second, the choice of the words is an important consideration. Few writers, perhaps, would categorically state that the verbs "came" and "went" in the second piece are the most appropriate ones that could be found. Nevertheless, these verbs do have a quality of impact; both are one-syllable words, and as such are appropriate to the flash of lightning.

The point to be made with young writers is that many concrete factors are involved in determining appropriateness of word choice. One should not simply say, "I like that word better just because I like it better. That's my opinion, and nobody can say I'm wrong." This is the type of argument used occasionally by inexperienced beginners. You should always try to correct the thinking that suggests there are no "right answers" in English. It is important to demonstrate to pupils that most effective expression rests on a sound foundation of writing technique.

Appropriateness of word choice can be practised with such models as the "What is it?" exercise on page 16 of chapter 2. A piece such as the one on "lemon" (page 18), where the young writer first picked the word "round", and then changed it to "oval", shows that lessons are best learned in practice, not in theory.

Simplicity

Some of the most effective writing derives its strength from its simplicity. However, inexperienced writers, unless shown otherwise, tend to think that the longer the words and the more complicated the combinations they use, the better their expression. Show them examples of pieces whose impact comes from their simplicity. Consider, for example, this poem written about the region in the far north of Canada:*

---

* The poem is by Knud Rasmussen from the book *Beyond the High Hills.*

There is joy in
Feeling the warmth
Come to the great world,
And seeing the sun
Follow its old footprints
In the summer night.

There is fear in
Feeling the cold
Come to the great world,
And seeing the moon
Follow its old footprints
In the winter night.

Most of the words in the above poem are of
single syllables, and certainly none of them is
complicated. The writer achieves his effect
partly through parallelism, and partly through
simple repetition.

Ask the pupils, too, to read this poem by a
ten-year-old boy from Canada. He had just
been out for a walk in the snow on a bright
day, and had been concentrating on the
shadows that he saw.

Shadows swaying to and fro,
Could be anything,
I don't know.

Look like monsters,
Under the window–
I don't know.

Look like witches
Flying low–
I don't know.

Shadows swaying to and fro,
Could be anything,
I don't know.

(F.J., St. John's School, Selkirk, Canada)

Simplicity of expression does not mean lack of meaning or feeling. In fact, the simple, concise piece often has the greatest impact. For example:

Winter
I feel the winter come;
I hear the winter cry;
I see the winter, numb
And sense the summer die.
(T.L., University of Toronto School, Toronto, Canada)

Blindness*
My eyes are in darkness all the time:
My fingers are my sun.
(G.S., Montreal West High School, Montreal, Canada)

Star
My light has travelled centuries to meet your eye —
And you don't even stop to wonder.
(T.V., Putney School, Putney, U.S.A.)

The process of re-writing usually reduces original expression to a simpler and more effective form. (This process is outlined in more detail in the section immediately following.) Although the first version of the poem below is only seventeen words in length, the polished final version of eight words satisfied its author better.

Night (1)
In the darkness of the night,
I feel the silence everywhere:
There is no other song here.

**Night (2) ** **
In the night,
Silence –
And no other song.

---

* This piece was written in Braille by a pupil who had been blind since the age of eight.

** This poem was recently published in the volume *A Compass of Open Veins* by the young Canadian poet, Grant Johnson.

Pupils in developing countries often write with a simplicity that borders on the primitive. Because they do not have an extensive vocabulary on which to draw, they do not clutter their expression with magniloquence and circumlocution. Look at this poem written by a young boy from New Guinea:

Follow the Track
Come away this way –
Hurry, let us go:
This is the way to go;
This is the path to follow.

Follow, follow the track;
Though it is steep and rugged;
Never, never turn back,
Or try to look behind.
(C.P., Garoka High School, Garoka, New Guinea)

Re-writing

Perhaps the most important stage in the creative process is the re-writing. Pupils must be taught that re-assessing and polishing their original expression is essential. In fact, professional writers do much of their most effective work *after* they have written their first versions.

Consider the following poem written by a young American girl on a yesterday/today/tomorrow theme. Mary worked on this piece for over a week, producing four different versions of the last two lines.

Once I walked
Unknowing:
Now aware of
beauty;
(1) Free to experience   (2) Free to enjoy
         Life   Living

| (3) Able to find Truth | (4) Able to seek Truth |

(M.M., Lyndon Institute, Lyndonville, U.S.A.)

Her change from the first to the second versions is an improvement. "Living" is a more appropriate word for the context than "life", and "enjoy" has a liveliness that "experience" lacks. The change from the third to the fourth version of the verbs "find" and "seek" is also an improvement.

Apart from altering the tone of a piece, re-writing frequently improves its clarity. First versions by the inexperienced, written in the white heat of enthusiasm, are often loose and tend to be wordy. Consider the following original piece:

Footprint in Mud (1)
Five deep semi-curved impressions
in a melted chocolate bar of mud,
and a thick club confronting the
five holes in descending order.

(K.L., Phillips Exeter Academy, Exeter, U.S.A.)

On re-consideration, the writer felt it would be best to omit the last two lines altogether. Then thinking about the rhythm, he decided to eliminate both "semi-curved" and "melted", which gave him the following final version:

Footprint in Mud (2)
Five deep impressions
In a chocolate bar of mud.

The change in the position of a single word can often have a significant influence on a piece.*

---

* David McCord makes a similar comment (page 92) about his poem "Tiger Lily" when he refers to the line, "its tongue is the velvet pretty anther."

Look at the following poem on winter, noticing in particular the final line:

Winter
Somewhere the dirt-grey snow
  and cloud-grey sky meet;
There is nothing else
Except the unmoving, black tree.
(P.K., Dunton High School, Montreal, Canada)

The final line has the rhythm and feel of prose. Hence the writer changed the position of one word in the line, and in so doing transformed it into a line of poetry:

Except the black, unmoving tree.

Notice how this alteration creates a natural rhythm break between the words "black" and "unmoving". It also shifts the emphasis of the line onto the adjective "unmoving", a change appropriate to the static mood of the poem as a whole.

Re-writing, especially when it is done by young pupils, generally has the effect of reducing the length of the original, and hence of strengthening it. This four-line piece is the product of five re-writings, and has more impact than the nine-line original:

Dull grey grass:
Rich soupy mud:
Three limp worms—
All drowned on the lawn.
(C.B., Repton School, Derbyshire, England)

Chapter 5 Approaches To Form II:

Forms Which Emphasize Images

In chapter 2 a number of form suggestions were presented which concentrated on the use of the single word in context. In this chapter the emphasis will progress to combinations of words (completed images) and to short pieces of two to six lines in length. Conciseness will continue to be an aim in each exercise, as will tightness of expression. Let me emphasize again, however, that the order in which the form models are presented is only a suggested one. Teachers should use them in any sequence they feel best fulfils the needs of their classes and pupils.

Single Image

Ask the pupils to think of any situation – probably something descriptive will serve best – and then to typify it in a single image through reference to some concrete situation. Consider this example by Basho, the famous Japanese poet:

Autumn evening–
A crow on a bare branch.

In this piece, Basho first sets the scene: autumn evening. He then tries to present in a single definite image the most characteristic thing about his topic, the item that makes it real for him. He chooses the starkness of a crow on a bare branch. Here are several other examples written by pupils:

A secluded pond–
The sound of a diving frog.

(P.M., St. Johnsbury Academy, St. Johnsbury, U.S.A.)

A warm kitchen–
The smell of roasted chicken.

(T.V., Dorval High School, Montreal, Canada)

Winter morning –
Icicles hanging heavy from the roof.

(T.M., Neelin High School, Brandon, Canada)

Rush hour –
Horns honking, lights flashing, people running.

(K.S., Horace Mann School, New York, U.S.A.)

Mini-skirts –
Stocking runs showing.

(A.B., Dunton High School, Montreal, Canada)

Battlefield –
Swirling dust against barbed-wire fences.

(T.S., Normanhurst High School, Sydney, Australia)

This exercise demands close observation and tight expression. Encourage your pupils to involve as many of their senses as they can in writing their pieces.

What Is It?

In a similar model in chapter 2 (page 16), pupils were introduced to a form which consisted of a number of single adjectives, each used to describe one of the five senses. The pupils wrote down their adjectives first, and withheld the subject until the last line of their piece. Try the same exercise again, only this time ask them to write a phrase or short clause about each sense, rather than a single word. Let them try to guess each other's topics, and thereby test the appropriateness of the writing. They may present the senses in any order they see fit. For example:

Sight: Yellow, flowing gold;
Smell: Clover-rich smell;
Taste: Soft warm ooze on my tongue;
Touch: Heavy, sticky liquid stream:
Subject: Honey.

(T.S., Winchester College, Winchester, England)

and:

Flashing colored lights;
Smoke and sweaty smell;
Distorted Dylan music,
Long hair and way-out gear;
Disco.

(C.E., North Ryde High School, Sydney, Australia)

Black smelling clouds of smoke;
Hot as cloth on fire;
Grating, crumbling awful taste;
Burnt Toast.

(C.C., Phillips Exeter Academy, Exeter, U.S.A.)

Stands straight and spindly;
Coarse, sand-paper feeling;
Smells like strong incense;
Grass green all its life,
Pine Tree.

(T.S., West Hill High School, Montreal, Canada)

Both hot and cold;
Sweet and sticky;
Melts in your mouth;
Mountain-shaped,
Hot Fudge Sundae.

(G.M., Msgr. Doran High School, Montreal, Canada)

As an extension of this model, pupils might
concentrate their images on one of the senses
only. In the following example the young
writer uses sounds exclusively:

Tinkling of glass,
Grating of iron,
Splintering of wooden beams,
Screeching of steel on steel,
Demolition Bulldozer.

(B.P., Bilton Grange School, Dunchurch, England)

Ideograms

The aim of this model is to create an accurate representation, in words, of either a number or a letter of the alphabet. The writer must make his description in three lines or less, and should be as precise as possible. The class may try to guess the symbol, either number or letter, after hearing each piece. What symbols do the following pieces describe?

A hump-backed man sitting down,
His head looking at the ground.
(M.W., Wager High School, Montreal, Canada)
Answer: C

The footprint of a bird in snow
When he is missing his middle toe.
(T.P., Ross School, Moose Jaw, Canada)
Answer: Y

A question seated
Or a proud bird's neck.
(May Swenson)
Answer: 2

A balloon flying
At the top of a string in the wind.
(T.R., Monklands High School, Montreal, Canada)
Answer: 9

If any of the pupils can write in a language, such as Chinese, which has different symbols from English, he might try to describe these symbols in English. The following examples were written by Chinese pupils at Raffles Institution in Singapore. Let the pupils try to construct the symbols as they hear their description.

A long thick mustache,
Or a Sherlock Holmes cap with a hole in the top.

   (eight)

A man with four hands and no head.

   (sky)

A TV aerial above a roof;
Above the aerial
Soars a bird into the distance.

   (god)

A table on top of a stone;
A box on top of the table;
A plate on top of the box;
A stick sticking into the plate.

   (high)

Three men balanced on a pole,
Or an 'E' that looks at the sky.

   (mountain)

Simile Structure

A useful introduction to figurative language may
be made through the simile. For example, you
might give a series of exercises in which pupils
write similes appropriate to any number of
everyday items, such as thunder, heat, happiness,
ice-cream cone, and so on. Insist on accuracy
in the choice of images, and warn beginners
against the use of clichés. Once pupils understand the simile, they might try a five-line poem
which has the following pattern:

Similes: Ears like towels flapping on the line;
          Legs like tree stumps;
          Tail like rope, and nose like a hose;

Action: When he trumpets, the jungle shakes –

Subject: Elephant.

(M.W., Public School, Harbour Island, Bahamas)

The first three lines in this model are similes, each
one describing some outstanding characteristic
of the subject. The fourth line is also a descriptive
one –not a simile, however – concentrating on
some action of the subject. The final line simply
names the subject. Encourage the class to guess
each other's topics as the work is read aloud,
(without the final line, of course). If a pupil has
chosen appropriate similes, his classmates
should be able to guess correctly.

Sharp as a dagger;
Cold as the snow;
Clear like glass;
Glistening, melting in the sunlight –
Icicle.

(M.N., John Rennie High School, Montreal, Canada)

Barracuda
Eyes like an eagle;
Tail like a propeller;
Teeth like a knife;
He slashes through the water –
Barracuda.

(E.J., St. Benedict's School, Harbour Island, Bahamas)

Tiger
Eyes like glowing embers;
Fur like coal and fire;
Jaws as hard as rows of knives;

When he walks, everything hides—
Tiger.
(I.S., St. Paul's School, Darjeeling, India)

"I Like Sounds"

All writing, whether prose or poetry, should have rhythm, as everything in life has rhythm. One cannot do anything—walk down the street, drive a car, or play a sport—without involving some kind of rhythm. Young writers should be aware of this important element of life and try to capture it in their work.

As an exercise, ask each pupil to start a piece with the words, "I like sounds". Then in the body of the piece, four to six lines, he may simply detail sounds which, to him, are appealing. He ends the piece with the same three words as began it. As pupils gain a knowledge of some of the sound devices—alliteration, onomatopeia, assonance, internal rhyme, and so on—they may incorporate them into their writing.

I like sounds—
The crisp sound of paper,
The rustling of corn,
The roar of a river,
The jingle of money,
I like sounds.
(P.C., Sydney Grammar School, Sydney, Australia)

I like sounds—
The sound of the tide as it rolls onto shore;
The cantering of horses on a cobble-stone road;
The pinging of furnace pipes,
The croacking of frogs,
The beat of rock music,
I like sounds.
(P.L., Riverdale High School, Montreal, Canada)

I like sounds–
The crackling of the fire on a cold winter night;
The grinding of a sports car as it slips into reverse;
The squeaking of boots on a snow-covered road;
The clanging of the Friday bell at 3:31;
I like sounds.

(N.B., Neelin High School, Brandon, Canada)

I like sounds–
Truck sounds,
Train sounds,
People-talking sounds,
Men-fixing-car sounds,
Building-a-building sounds,
I like sounds.

(F.P., Crown Woods Comprehensive School, London, England)

A Colour Personified

Ask the pupils to pick a colour and try to make it
come alive in words. In order to do so, they should
compose five lines, each line relating the colour
to one of the five senses. For example, if a pupil
is thinking about the colour red, he must put
down images for the sight of red, its sound, taste,
touch, and smell. He should pick his images with
care, choosing ones that, to him, best typify his
colour. The order in which he presents the sense
images is up to him, and he need not refer to
every sense if he finds one or two particularly
difficult, or inappropriate. After all the pupils in
the class have written about their colour, they
might enjoy trying to identify each others,

The grasp of the greedy,
A pie crust,
Metal dropping on metal,
The flash of a gypsy's earring,
Sweet cider,
Gold.

(V.A., Repton School, Derbyshire, England)

The eye of a cat,
Go,
Sickness of the sea,
A salad of weeds,
Green.

(D.D., Philaemon Wright School, Hull, Canada)

A pumpkin's bright gaiety;
Burning flames of fire;
Autumn in the warm sun;
A slurping sound when eating;
Orange.

(L.N., Lyndon Institute, Lyndonville, U.S.A.)

Fire engines roaring down the street;
Danger;
Hot, as the summer sun;
Sweet, juicy, and crunchy;
Red.

(M.K., St. George's School, Montreal, Canada)

Juicy ripe plums,
The fragrance of blooming violets;
A velvety touch,
Trumpets sounding,
A colour for the royal family –
Purple.

(C.R., Hull Elementary School, Hull, Canada)

Fresh spring earth,
The squeaking of rusty railroad-car wheels;
The taste of melted chocolate;
Well-done steak,
Brown.

(L.N., Pittwater House Grammar School, Sydney, Australia)

Once the pupils have some experience with this
form, they should be able to produce some
surprisingly appropriate images.

Four-Line Synonym Model

Pupils should seek alternative word choices for
any context. They must learn that the first word

that jumps into their mind is not necessarily the best one. Serious consideration of various possibilities – taking into account mood, tone, intended emphasis, and so on – generally produces a more satisfactory choice.

In this regard, a study of synonyms is always useful. (Pupils should also be made aware of the value of the thesaurus, and instructed in its use.) Ask the pupils to compose a four-line piece in which the first and last lines are synonyms, and the middle two lines – short phrases or clauses – detail specific instances of the subject. For example:

Solitude –
A quiet mountain cave;
A garden late at night;
Loneliness.

(L.G., Punahou School, Honolulu, Hawaii)

Pupils may notice that the second and third lines represent what the writer considers to be vivid examples or concrete images of his subject, "solitude". The final word, "loneliness", is intended to mirror the spirit of the subject, yet at the same time add a further dimension to it.

Here are a number of other examples of this model:

Anger
Wind-lashed trees;
A howling child;
Fury.

(G.M., Friends School, Hobart, Australia)

Security –
An extra twenty cents;

A new thing;
Safety.
(A.B., Loretto Convent,
Normanhurst, Australia)

Rabble—
A weak master;
A dormitory after lights-out;
A stir.
(A.C., St. Ignatius Riverview School,
Sydney, Australia)

Excitement—
A fast-beating heart;
Noisy voices;
Joy.
(H.W., Cardinal Newman School, Montreal, Canada)

Portrait Of A Month

Ask the pupils to present in three lines or less a portrait of any month of the year. They may not mention the month in the body of their piece, but must give features of it so that the reader can identify it. Accuracy of detail is important here. Remember, too, that the authencity of the description hinges on the place to which the writer is referring. Seasons are reversed in the northern and southern hemispheres, and if an Australian pupil is to make a sensible guess about a month described by a North American, he must take this fact into account. Here are a number of examples. Let the pupils try to guess the month described.

October
Squashes and pumpkins are set on the step;
Turkeys and partridges hang in the shed;
Colours of green turn orange and red.
(M.H., Lyndon Institute, Lyndonville, Vermont, U.S.A.)

May

A painter has splashed the trees;
The mornings and evenings close in;
Frost creeps like a white disease onto the land.

(M.B., The King's School, Parramatta,
New South Wales, Australia)

August

Lanterns in the dark;
Dumplings on a string;*
Humidity.

(T.B., Raffles Institution, Singapore)

February

Blustery winds slashing your face;
Blinding snow quickens your pace,
Wheels of cars spin on the ice.

(M.S., Monklands High School, Montreal, Canada)

January

Trains that are ovens;
Skies that are red;
Shirts that stick.

(S.M., Sydney Grammar School, Sydney, Australia)

November

Sitting silent under the empty birches,
Cold night settles on the frosted leaves.

(D.C., Phillips Exeter Academy,
Exeter, New Hampshire, U.S.A.)

December

Heat that makes the blue leaves wilt;
Heat that shrivels drift-sand dry;
Still, endless day.

(J.W., Downlands College,
Toowoomba, Queensland, Australia)

May

Eagerly the trout rises to the new hatch of flies;
Piercingly the redshank calls;
Fresh is the breeze which carries the pollen.

(A.A., Foremark School, Derbyshire, England)

---

* A part of a traditional feast in South-East Asia.

March
A grey mist hangs over the hill tops –
The rain comes down;
My trees are grey.

(J.L., St. Edmund's School,
Canterbury, England)

Adverb Model

Ask the pupils to write a poem in which each line starts with an adverb. They may pick any adverb they wish as long as they retain it throughout. They might try several pieces, varying the adverbs they select to alter the intention of their writing. James Reeves has provided a useful model with his poem "Slowly". Notice that he writes in rhymed couplets. You may have your pupils do the same.

Slowly the tide creeps up the sand;
Slowly the shadows cross the land;
Slowly the cart-horse pulls his mile;
Slowly the old man mounts the stile.

Slowly the hands move round the clock;
Slowly the dew dries on the dock;
Slow is the snail – but slowest of all,
The green moss spreads on the old brick wall.

Reeves breaks the pattern in the final two lines. However, it is probably best if pupils do not, for the sake of uniformity. Here are three other examples. The one entitled "angrily" is chiefly narrative in intent.

Quickly
Quickly planes sweep across the sky;
Quickly a man does up his tie;
Quickly trains speed across the land;
Quickly the sun turns mud to sand;

Quickly the rains fall from the sky;
Quickly my brother bolts his pie;
Quickly the boats steam through the sea;
Quickly time seems to be going for me.

(J.S., Dunton High School, Montreal, Canada)

Lightly
Lightly fall the snowflakes on the ground;
Lightly comes sleep on its midnight round;
Lightly the cat curls up by the fire;
Lightly fall the leaves – autumn's attire;
Lightly comes the fog on muffled feet;
Lightly come sun's rays – daytime's heat.

(N.H., Lyndon Institute, Lyndonville, U.S.A.)

Angrily
Angrily the leopard fought;
Angrily in the net was caught;
Angrily the men drew near;
Angrily she roared in fear;
Angrily she was placed in a cage;
Angrily her mind was enraged;
Angrily she did her act;
Angrily the long whip cracked.

(S.S., Northmount High School, Montreal, Canada)

Make A Word Live

Ask the pupils to think of any word in the language, and to write about it in four or five lines which make it come alive for the reader. The writer must provide accurate representations of his word in order to give it a living personality. He should include reference to the senses, or to colours, weather, actions, or anything that will help to identify it. Let the pupils try to guess the words their classmates personify.

Dirty eraser;
Blotched page;
Tear streaks;

Despair in the air;
Examination.

(J.P., Philaemon Wright High School, Hull, Canada)

Tangled greenery
Mysterious and dark;
A haunting cry-
Then silence-
Jungle.

(J.N., Riverdale High School, Montreal, Canada)

A throbbing ache,
A dullness of the mind;
Glazed eyes that see no joy;
A bloated, gnawing stomach;
Hunger.

(M.A., Putney School, Putney, U.S.A.)

Black and gooey;
Useful, yet a nuisance;
Impossible thing,
Maddening-never gives up:
Tar.

(S.W., Crown Woods Comprehensive School,
London, England)

A smile-
Gaiety, laughter, bells ringing:
Sunshine, warmth,
A dancing clown.
Happiness.

(T.M., Brisbane Grammar School, Brisbane, Australia)

A deathly presence;
A coiled flash,
A convulsive flex,
Frozen silence-
Snake.

(J.G., Dorval High School, Montreal, Canada)

"I Like That Stuff"

The poet Adrian Mitchell has written a form
of poem which serves as a useful model for

humorous expression. Each verse has four
lines. Here are several of his pieces:

Lovers lie around in it;
Broken glass is found in it;
Grass,
I like that stuff.

Tuna fish get trapped in it;
Ladies legs come wrapped in it:
Nylon,
I like that stuff.

Carpenters make cots of it;
Undertakers use lots of it;
Wood,
I like that stuff.

In this model, the third line is a single noun
which names the subject. The fourth line is
always the same; "I like that stuff". The first
two lines conclude with a variety of two
word endings, such as with it, by it, on it, in
it. There should be an internal rhyme in these
lines just before the last two words; in the
examples above, it is found in "around" and
"found"; "trapped" and "wrapped"; "cots" and
"lots".

Pupils seem to enjoy experimenting with this
model, and produce a wide range of pieces in
the process.

Bread oozes with gobs of it;
Knives are covered with blobs of it;
Peanut butter,
I like that stuff.

(P.W., Macdonald High School,
Montreal, Canada)

Old sea dogs string miles of it;
Kittens tie up piles of it;

Yarn,
I like that stuff.

(M.T., Royal Arthur School,
Montreal, Canada)

Barbers make money mowing it;
Boys work hard at growing it;
Hair,
I like that stuff.

(J.R., Friends School, Hobart, Australia)

Teeth often get stuck in it;
Dentists are in luck with it;
Toffee,
I like that stuff.

(R.M., Phillips Exeter Academy,
Exeter, U.S.A.)

Careless rumps are found in it;
Clean new shoes are ground in it;
Bubble gum,
I like that stuff.

(P.W., Repton School,
Derbyshire, England)

A variation of this form can be produced by
ending the four-line verse with the words, "I
hate that stuff".

Four-Line Sensory Model

Ask the pupils to make a four-line piece which
concentrates on any two of the senses; the
two which they feel are most characteristic
of the subject they have chosen. (This exercise
should help pupils to focus their sense experiences
as they write.) The form goes as follows:

Trains –
A rumble of wheels,
A rush of air,
Trains.

(P.S., Warwick, Australia)

The first and last lines simply state the subject.
The middle two lines–they may be phrases,
clauses, or any concise combination of
words–highlight outstanding sense aspects of
the subject. The boy who wrote the piece
above lived in a country town where only two
trains passed by each day. He was particularly
taken with their sound, and by the sucking
sensation they produced as they roared past
the platform.

Other examples:

Bubble gum–
A stretchy piece of goo,
An endless dinner,
Bubble gum.

(T.S., Outremont High School,
Montreal, Canada)

Go-karts–
A shaking in the handle-bars;
A rumble of pistons;
Go-karts.

(J.S., Bellevue Hill Primary School,
Sydney, Australia)

Rockets–
A cloud of smoke;
A roar of power;
Rockets.

(M.M., Bishop's College School,
Lennoxville, Canada)

Garbage cans–
A foul reeking;
A buzzing of flies;
Garbage cans.

(R.J., Sydney Grammar School,
Sydney, Australia)

Master–
A bellow of rage;
A hail of chalk;
Master.

(T.M., The Dragon School,
Oxford, England)

Brumbies*–
A rush of hooves;
A flying of stones;
Brumbies.

(L.M., Brisbane Grammar School,
Brisbane, Australia)

Modern art–
A feast of optical delusions;
A psychedelic explosion of color;
Modern art.

(J.G., Newton High School,
Newton, U.S.A.)

Optic Variations

Young writers generally enjoy experimenting with the structure of their poems. They should be encouraged to do so, because form is one of the elements of poetry with which they should be familiar. Give them a number of variations, and let them make up one or more of their own following each model. A first suggestion might be the straight optic piece, a poem made in the shape of whatever it represents:

home sweet home home sweet home home sweet home home sweet home home sweet home home sweet home no Negroes, Chinese or Jews allowed in this building home sweet home sweet home home sweet home home sweet home home

This poem, written by a fourteen-year old, second-generation Canadian, depicts an apple with a worm crawling into it, a worm which will eventually infect the apple.

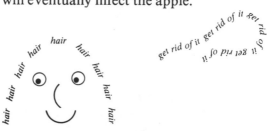

(T.M., Putney School, Putney, U.S.A.)

Optic poems can contain humour. The one above, by a thirteen-year-old boy, depicts a head of long hair, over which hangs a pair of scissors formed by the repeated words, "get rid of it".

Ladder Variation

The following piece, written in the shape of steps of a ladder, presents an interesting model, particularly in an age where so much emphasis is placed on getting to the top.

```
        President, Chairman of the Board
         'Yes, Sir'
          Color Television Console,
          Cadillac,
           Exclusive Club,
          Rotary Club,
          Country Club,
         Vice-President, Sales Manager,
          'Yes, Sir'
        haircut and shave,
       degree,
     college (ivy)
```

(G.G., Belmont Hill School, Boston, U.S.A.)

Skinny poem

Lou Lipsitz has given us a model which
contains one word only per line, and hence
runs straight down the page. He appropriately
calls his creation "skinny poem".

Skinny
poem
all
your
ribs
showing
even
without
a
deep
breath
thin
legs
rotted
with
disease
Live
here!
on
this
page
barely
making
it
like
the
mass
of
mankind.

Scrabble poetry

The word game *Scrabble* has gained
international popularity with young and old

alike. Ask pupils to make up a poem where
the letters are inter-meshed as they are in a
completed game of scrabble.

```
P
E
RUSHING
S        O
O        I
N        NOWHERE
S        G H
           A
             THEIR
        D SU
      KNOW R
         N  R
         THEY
```

(T.S., Bishop's College School,
Lennoxville, Canada)

The almost circular, following-its-own-tail
shape of this scrabble poem is particularly appropriate to the message its writer is trying to
convey.

Acrostic pieces

Ask the pupils to make an acrostic poem,
which has the letters of a word written down
the page on the left. Each of the letters
serves to start one of the succeeding lines.

Warmth is gone;
Inside there's chill;
No relief anywhere
To the cold blasts:
Eat your heart out;
Relief is not in sight.

(B.P., Henley Grammar School,
Henley, England)

Make up Your Own

Once the pupils have done these five variations, they should try to devise some further optic ideas of their own.

Four-Line Descriptive Model

Ask the pupils to study this four-line descriptive model:

subway train,
stuffed with people,
slices the darkness,
sleekly.

They will notice that the first line simply names the subject of the piece, which may be anything. The second line, a phrase or a clause, gives a visual description of the subject. The third line, again a short phrase or clause, describes the action of the subject by telling what it normally does. The final line is a single word, an adverb, carefully chosen to catch the spirit of the subject. Each of the four lines starts with the same letter, thus providing a type of unity through sound.

In some respects, this model serves as a review of several others previously attempted. Here, too, pupils need to observe carefully in order to write well. They must pick their words, particularly their adverbs, with discrimination in order to capture the mood of their subject.

Jello
Jello,
Jammed with light,
Jewelledly glistening,
Jingly.
(J.B., York House School,
Vancouver, Canada)

Fish
Fish,
Finely colored,
Finning and flicking,
Furiously.

(M.O., Raffles Institution,
Singapore)

Parrots
Parrots,
Poised on poles,
Preen their feathers,
Proudly.

(R.W., Howrah Primary School,
Hobart, Australia)

Tugboat
Tugboat,
Towing a barge,
Travelling the waters,
Tirelessly.

(B.S., Shawnigan Lake School,
Shawnigan Lake, Canada)

Highway
Highway,
Hurtles across the prairie,
Heading somewhere,
Headlong.

(S.M., Neelin High School,
Brandon, Canada)

Mountain
Mountain,
Maimed by man,
Motioning upward,
Majestically.

(J.B., St. Paul's School,
Darjeeling, India)

Variety In Line Structure

An important element in the construction of
any piece is variety. Repetition of a pattern, if

it is overdone, can lead to monotony. Ask the pupils to make a poem with the following form*:

Bombers
Gripping the sky with metal wings,
They fly;
Sighting their prey with cruel eyes,
They fall;
Dropping their loads of spitting steel,
They climb;
Fleeing the clouds of smoke and fire,
They run.

(N.J., Canberra Grammar School,
Canberra, Australia)

The first line, and every alternate line thereafter, begins with a participle. (The opportunity arises here for a lesson on verbals, and the dual function of the participle as both adjective and verb.) Every second line consists of two words only, a personal pronoun followed by a verb in the present tense. This model also introduces pupils to the idea of variety in line length, and thus provides diversity for reader and writer alike.

Pupils may alter their pronouns and their tenses as long as they retain proper balance throughout their pieces. Here is an example of this model written by a young Canadian girl. The words in bold type could well be the subject of a discussion on the most appropriate word for the context.

The Wind
Hurtling across the **wind-capped** waves,
It **roars**;
Sweeping over the **uneven** sands,

* My thanks to Bruce McPherson, an imaginative young Australian
  teacher of English, for this suggestion.

It **pierces**;
Ripping through the **naked** trees,
It **cuts**;
Rumbling into the **engulfing** fog,
It **dies**.

(D.G., York House School,
Vancouver, Canada)

Three-Line Reaction Model

Ask each pupil to make a three-line piece with
the following pattern: The first line is the
subject – a single word, phrase, or clause – on
any topic of the pupil's choice. The second
line details the action of the subject by means
of a verb, verbal phrase, or clause. The final
line gives the reaction of the writer to his
subject in a word or phrase. In order to create
a strand of unity through sound, ask the pupils
to begin each of their three lines with the same
letter.

The major emphasis with this model should
be on the writer's reaction. Hence he should
know what he wants to say before trying to
write it.

Dogs
Dogs,
Dashing everywhere,
Daring adventurers.

(I.E., Newington College,
Sydney, Australia)

Friday
Friday,
Forever lingers on,
Frustrating.

(S.N., West Hill High School,
Montreal, Canada)

Chimneys
Chimneys,
Churning out smoke,
Choking the air.

(E.D., Horace Mann School,
New York, U.S.A.)

Mini-skirts
Mini-skirts;
Maxi-legs;
Messy.

(K.W., Monklands High School,
Montreal, Canada)

Pigeons
Pigeons,
Pecking,
Purposeful business.

(M.W., Cranbrook School,
Sydney, Australia)

Prose/Telegram

Pupils sometimes feel that the more they write, the better their work. Perhaps this thinking developed in the time of stipulated word totals ("Write 3000 words about such-and-such."), when not to achieve a certain number of words was, in part, to fail the assignment.

You should stress the point that in writing, quantity does not necessarily mean quality; in fact, it often means the reverse. As an exercise in conciseness of expression, ask the pupils to write four or five lines of prose, or a short paragraph if they wish, on any subject of their choice. Let them start this exercise without any preamble as to its aim.

As an example, here is what one girl in Tasmania produced:

The world spun. I was swallowed by
the liquid blue. Movement became
easy as I lay suspended on my back.
Crystal spheres danced up past my
eyes, and burst out of the blue,
breaking the solid silver ceiling, and
spreading ripples across the surface
above. (45 words)

(J.H., Friends School, Hobart, Australia)

After the pupils have finished their prose, ask
them to imagine that they are sending a
telegram to a friend. In this telegram they are
to include the main details covered in their
piece of prose. The telegram is going to cost
them ten cents a word, so economy of
expression, and hence finance, is important.
Don't tell the pupils about this part of the
exercise before they start their prose, or it
will influence their writing in the first part.
Perhaps the lesson that will strike home for
most pupils is how loosely they expressed
themselves in their original paragraph. Faced
with the demands of the telegram, the
Australian girl quoted above reduced her 45
words of prose to the following three: *Went
scuba-diving.*

This exercise should provide a variety of
useful writing activities. For example, each
pupil might read his paragraph aloud, while
the others in the class write an appropriate
telegram to go with it. This discipline serves
a similar function to writing a *précis*.

Here is another example of the prose/telegram
model:

I come home from school feeling
really low. Nothing—nothing at all
has gone right today. I sit on my
bed wallowing in self-pity. Suddenly
my guitar catches my eye. I start to
strum: I start to sing. I doodle
around, and my sorrows vanish. A
song is born. (50 words)

Came home feeling low:
Saw my guitar, started to strum.
Wrote a song. Felt better. (16 words)

(I.W., Raffles Institution, Singapore)

Making A Poem

Suggest to your pupils that putting a poem
together is like assembling a model. Remind
them of the kits for airplanes, racing cars, and
so on. You begin by putting all the parts out
on the floor. Then you read the instructions
and follow them step by step until all the pieces
are assembled.

Ask the pupils to make a poem in a similar
way, paying attention to the details of its
construction. They should start by dividing a
page in their writing books into two sections
by drawing a line down the middle. Over the
left-hand section they should put the heading
senses (i.e., sight, sound, smell, taste, touch);
over the right-hand section *feelings, moods,
reactions*. Ask them to pick any topic on
which they would like to write, and put down
under each heading anything that comes to
mind about their subject. They should work
quickly, not taking more than three or four
minutes. They may simply jot down ideas –
phrases or even single words.

The pupils now have on their papers the parts
of a poem, like the parts of a model. However,
they are probably not in any particular order.
Now ask the pupils to look at their parts
again carefully, think about their order, and
try to put them together to make a short
poem of approximately six to eight lines in
length.

Notice how the following poem by a thirteen-
year-old boy is constructed. First come his
jottings about his toothache and the dentist's
office:

Senses	**Feelings, moods, reacti**
Pain everywhere	"Is it very sore?" – denti
Like fingernails pulled out	Office so unsympatheti
Uncomfortable	Pain
Red-hot pain in mouth	Agony
Tooth dying	"How sorry" – nurse
Sitting in dentist's office	Will it ever end?
Hurt right to my toes	Never before as bad
Like match-sticks burning	Can I take it?

From these parts he put together the following
poem:

Tooth Ache
Here I sit in the dentist's office –
Trying to bear the pain
As my tooth dies,
And all anyone can say is:
"I'm so sorry", or "Does it hurt?"
Does it hurt to have your fingernails pulled out?
Or matches burning between your toes?
I've never known pain until now.

(R.A., Monklands High School,
Montreal, Canada)

Through exercises such as this one, pupils
may be helped to realize that writing is a craft

involving specific skills which can be developed with practice. Making a poem is not a mysterious process achieved by only a few. It is something that anyone can attempt, and that all can benefit from trying.

Chapter 6   What Makes A Teacher?

Teaching is an art. Since each teacher is unique, teaching must, therefore, be an individual, largely personal art. As a teacher gains experience, he develops his understanding of himself, of his pupils, and hence of his own most effective *modus operandi*. In considering teaching, then, one should recognize that there are no absolutes either of method or of performance. Each person must be true to himself in trying to develop his potential as a professional.

However, certain characteristics are generally recognized as important in the make-up of any teacher. Attempting to choose the most important of these characteristics is a subjective process, and individual teachers obviously differ in the factors they propose. At the prompting of a number of colleagues, and with considerable hesitation because of the nature of the task, let me suggest twelve characteristics for the consideration of other teachers. They are proposed not as a type of model, but as areas of development of which every teacher should be aware.* I shall divide these characteristics into two broad categories, personal and professional.

Personal Characteristics

"Depth of Person"

This characteristic is difficult to put into words because it is concerned with what might be called "the things of the spirit". The man

* It should be noted here that every adult is, in effect, a teacher, whether in his own home with his own children, or simply in his community as he goes about his daily tasks. Therefore, I hope that these proposals are of interest to all adults, not just for professional teachers.

who has depth of person has the ability to move outside the perimeter of his own self-concern and become involved in the concerns of those around him. He has a capacity for sharing, for taking an interest in the interests of others, and for seeing the "people possibilities" in any situation. The man with depth of person has warmth and maturity which inspires confidence in young and old alike. He has kindness, patience, and a capacity for friendship. In short, he understands.

Belief in the Potential of Each Individual

A teacher should try to develop (if he does not possess it in the first instance) a belief in the potential of each one of his pupils. He should have confidence in their ability to tackle a situation and he should tell them so. Essentially a teacher is trying to help his pupils to discover themselves, and thus to earn self-respect.

Liking for Young People

A teacher should want to hear the ideas of young people, share in their experiences, and be involved with them regardless of the situation. If he is attuned to their interests, he should be able to help them bridge the gap between childhood and adulthood. A teacher must have an understanding of, and hence a sympathy for, what, to some people, may appear to be the idiosyncrasies of youth. He must like young people and if he does, then most other things have a chance of falling into place.

Enthusiasm for Living and Learning

As he hopes to set an example for the young,

a teacher should try to exhibit an enthusiasm for whatever he undertakes. He should be infused with a *joie de vivre* that is evident to others working with him. He should try to cultivate a range of interests and show a willingness to continue learning about his subject, about others, and about himself. A teacher should try to develop a staying power, as well as the ability to recharge himself for the challenges of each new day.

Courage and Conviction

In a time of rapidly changing values, a teacher must be ready to stand and be counted on matters of principle, regardless of criticism or unpleasant personal consequences. Unless teachers and parents give some guidance, young people are in danger of going adrift without a rudder. Adults must not lose their nerve when faced with stormy seas. Harold Loukes* compares giving direction to young people with steering a ship, and says, "The one route that's the wrong route, is not having a route at all".

Finding the right route presents difficulties for every adult. The Reverend Father Baker, Rector of Downlands College, Toowoomba, Australia, underlined the problem in a recent address when he commented: "The dilemma in educating adolescents today lies in the alternatives of too much or too little freedom. Whether we like it or not, we are preparing our young people to live in a permissive society where many of the old restraints have

* Harold Loukes is reader in Education at Oxford, and an internationally recognized authority on young people. (See chapter 7)

gone. It is education in the responsible use
of freedom that is so important today".

In addition to giving a positive lead to young
people, a teacher should be loyal to the colleagues with whom and for whom he works,
and, in particular, not be critical of others
behind their backs. A teacher should have the
courage to admit mistakes and the strength of
character to learn from them.

Sense of Humour

If a teacher doesn't have this quality he's in
trouble. It's hard to say what he can do
without it. He should try to cultivate the
ability to laugh at himself, and to see the
amusing or ridiculous side of any situation.
A light-hearted disposition is a great asset,
not just for Friday afternoons, but for every
day of the week. Any classroom period
without at least one hearty laugh cannot be
considered a complete success. Inspiration
often soars on wings of laughter.

Professional Characteristics*

Feeling For His Subject

A teacher should have a belief in the value of
his subject – whether it is grammar, Greek, or
geraniums – and of its relevance to himself and
his pupils. He should try to develop an enthusiasm for his work which serves to motivate
those around him. To paraphrase a familiar
expression, interest is usually caught, not taught.

---

* These characteristics may have less application for those who are not
  professional teachers. Parents and other adults should try to apply
  the suggestions relating to the classroom to their more general
  dealings with young people.

A teacher should seek to develop a command of his subject and hence have some solid knowledge to impart. Being one lesson ahead is not good enough. His scholarship, lightly carried, can serve to inspire his pupils to increase their own understanding of the subject. In addition, a teacher should always be trying to develop more effective ways of communicating his material. Yet his concern should be not only with subject matter, but also with the response of his pupils to it. He should try to make himself familiar with their abilities, stage of maturity, and present level of attainment in his subject. This means trying to develop a type of antenna which is attuned to his pupils, and specifically to their needs and moods of the moment.

Experienced teachers try to develop simplicity and clarity in their presentations almost in the Biblical sense of teaching in parables. This technique enables them to make complicated concepts appear easy. Facility in the technique can only result from a thorough understanding of the subject matter, and hence from an appreciation of its complexity.

While discussing method it is perhaps unnecessary, but nonetheless important, to suggest that every teacher should concentrate on being himself, and so become aware of and work with his personal strengths and weaknesses. This statement implies that there is no such thing in the teaching of any subject as *the* right method. There are as many effective teaching methods as there are individual effective teachers. Each teacher must be true to himself in developing his own style, which may be achieved by experimentation on the part of young teachers and by

continuing re-assessment on the part of more
mature teachers.

Energy and Hard Work

A teacher should try to exhibit an enthusiasm
for every job, and take the attitude that nothing
is too much trouble where the development of
human character is concerned. (He will probably
be able to do his work with greater vigour and
pleasure if he maintains a certain level of physical
fitness. The principle of *mens sana in corpore
sano* has proven valid since the time of the
Greeks.) The teacher should be dedicated to his
profession. As in any undertaking, when his
intention is right, there are few obstacles which
he cannot overcome by intelligently directed
hard work.

Sense of the Dramatic

A teacher should try to develop a feeling for
the positive tension that exists in every
situation; that is, the element of unpredict-
ability that makes every moment potentially
exciting. He should try to cultivate a sense
of timing much as stage professionals do. A
teacher should be able to find enjoyment in
acting and interacting with other people. Such
"acting" must always take place within a
framework of sincerity, however. Otherwise,
it will not ring true.

Ability to Manage the Situation

Every teacher should try to develop confidence
in himself—outward assurance and ease while he
is with young people. This attribute is based
partly on experience, and should increase as his
classroom experience grows. Effective teachers

often have a type of presence which, without being overpowering or unduly assertive, suggests command. Pupils can feel it. They have an almost intuitive way of knowing when a situation is under control. Nobody respects lack of order, least of all young people. A teacher should be ready to act if a pupil is not strong enough to discipline himself. Hence a teacher should try to be "tough" in expecting excellence and not accepting the slipshod, yet "tender" in being patient and understanding.

Innovative Capacity

The teacher should try to cultivate the ability to see the possibilities in any situation, and to develop his subject, and himself, in new or experimental ways. Educational advances seldom occur simply from following the book. Each teacher should try occasionally to break new ground. To do this, he must have a vision of what might be, and the courage to take the first step.

Chapter 7 Profiles Of Distinguished Teachers

In the hope of giving life to some of the characteristics discussed in the previous chapter, I shall attempt brief profiles of twelve distinguished teachers. It has been my privilege to work with them, as pupil or teacher, during the past thirty years. Their backgrounds are diverse; the group includes four Englishmen, three Australians, two Canadians, one American, one Scot, and one Asian. Their selection must be, of necessity, a personal one, and the assessments subjective. I offer the profiles, with apologies for their inadequacy, in the hope that reading about these teachers may guide and inspire others, as association with them has inspired me.

Father Athol Murray

Père is in his eighties now, but you'd never know it. He is as full of enthusiasm and belief in young people as he was when he first founded Notre Dame College in Wilcox, Saskatchewan, over forty years ago. He has always had faith in the young, and in the limitless possibilities for growth of the human spirit. He often speaks to his boys about the "unborn greatness" in every man, and his message gets across. He lights flames of ambition in them which continue to burn long after they have left this Canadian prairie town of three grain elevators and a handful of permanent inhabitants.

In many ways *Père* is the universal man. He reveres the Greeks and patterns much of his own thinking on the best that has come to us from the Golden Age. Yet at the same time, he is fully contemporary. Only last fall he had two bronze doors installed in his "Tower of God" – a structure built to the glory of all faiths –

depicting the astronauts walking on the moon.
Père is a realist as well as a visionary.

You wouldn't have to spend long with him to
recognize he is a character. *Reader's Digest* has
done a profile on him in their "most unforgetta-
ble" section. He chain smokes, letting the ashes
fall down the front of his shirt. He is often
unshaven. He speaks with disarming directness.
His bedroom-study usually appears to have just
been struck by a cyclone. These things really
don't matter to him, however. They are super-
ficial. Above them stands a man of the spirit
whose life has touched the lives of thousands
with its optimism and abundant love. Ask any
of his boys. They'll tell you.

Harold Loukes

Harold Loukes is currently reader in education
at Oxford University. Author of numerous
books, an eloquent and amusing speaker,
Harold Loukes has helped countless teachers-in-
training with his insights into the nature of
young people and his perceptive interpretations
of daily events. Although a scholar of considerable note, he has always sought the practical,
workable solution to any problem, rather than
the high-sounding, theoretical one. This is why
his ideas have been of enormous benefit to so
many teachers.

His understanding of his own students is
legendary. He always seems to be able to find
the right word of encouragement whenever
spirits are down. Although he is an active
Quaker, he seldom talks about his faith. He lives
it for all to see. Harold Loukes treats those he
meets with dignity. He makes everyone feel

important and earns widespread respect in return.

Bill Oats

Bill Oats is an Australian, a man who has been the Headmaster and inspiration force behind the Friends' School in Hobart, Tasmania for twenty-seven years now. Bill is a community leader, a man of wide experience who has touched the lives of many with his qualities of humour, humanity, and scholarship.

Perhaps the quality that most distinguishes Bill for me is his humility, and his respect for the dignity of every person with whom he meets. A member of his staff tells a story that illustrates this quality.

During the course of each week, Bill Oats takes every one of the pupils in his school for some subject or activity. He knows over nine hundred young people by name and nature. The five to seven year-olds he takes for singing. Sitting at the piano in the junior gymnasium, he introduces them to songs from many countries in many languages. Bill regards music as one of the best ways of expanding the soul–of helping each person to discover and develop his own inner self, and hence to grow as an individual.

One day not long ago–almost at the end of a school year in which Bill had been conducting his weekly musical sessions with the youngest members of the Friends' community–a truck driver drove his lorry into the school grounds. The driver had some goods to deliver, and stopped one of the six year-olds to ask for directions. The young pupil didn't know the answer, but as luck would have it, at that precise

moment, Bill Oats walked across the far side of
the school yard. One of the teachers on the
Friends' staff was sitting on a bench nearby,
having lunch. The teacher heard the driver say
to the child: "Who is that fellow walking across
there? Do you think he could help me?" The
pupil replied: "O, he's the man who plays the
piano and sings songs with us."

To me, this story typifies Bill Oats. One of the
most distinguished Headmasters in Australia,
his year-long relationship with this particular
child had not resulted in the pupil knowing
Bill's title, but rather in appreciating one of his
greatest loves. This type of communication
represents, to me, the essence of an
outstanding human being.

V.R. Mustard

"Musty" is over ninety now, but is still
active in a variety of hobbies and personal
involvements in Dover. He taught me when
I was thirteen years of age, and opened my
eyes to a range of interests I had never
considered before – Greek mythology, coin
collecting, ornithology, painting, and many
others. In those days "Musty" had been
teaching at Lower Canada College in Montreal
for more than forty years, yet he still had a
sparkle in his eye and a spring in his step. He
understood young boys, and treated each one
of us as his own. Sometimes we misbehaved
with him, but he seldom got cross and I
never once saw him lose his temper. He knew
that young boys were meant to have fun.
"Musty" was a man of warmth and sympathy,
a real Mr. Chips. He inspired me to become a
teacher.

Bill Connell

Bill Connell is professor of education at
Sydney University in New South Wales,
Australia. A writer of considerable force and
insight, Bill has long been a pioneer in the
field of international educational thought. He
has travelled widely; I first met him on a railway
carriage in Russia. Bill is an innovator in
whatever he does. Working with his own
students, he has a patient and perceptive
manner, and a skill at helping the individual
to find his own strengths and interests. This
is a rare talent. Bill doesn't impose himself
on others; rather he acts as the most positive
form of catalyst. Apart from his many
qualities as a teacher, Bill Connell is a
genuine person with a rich sense of humour, a
man who gains the affection and respect of
almost everyone he meets.

Steven Penton

Steven Penton, an Englishman and Oxford
graduate, has devoted most of his teaching
life to Lower Canada College in Montreal. He
was headmaster there for over a quarter of a
century, retiring only recently to write a history
of the school. He has always been a man of
distinguished presence, and an eloquent and
knowledgeable speaker on almost any topic.
He holds a great affection for his pupils and
takes a personal interest in their accomplishments, even years after they have left the
school. His chief qualities, perhaps, are his
loyalty to the school, his colleagues, and his
boys, and his devotion to duty. Unselfish, a
gentleman at all times, Steven Penton has

established through his own example standards of conduct which have influenced genera-
tions of Canadian young men.

Sir Arnold Plant

I shall never forget the first occasion on
which I met Sir Arnold. He was at that time
director of the post-graduate course in business
administration at the London School of
Economics. He walked into the seminar
room an erect and dignified figure smoking a
pipe, and gave our class, which was composed
of young, adult students from fifteen countries,
the first of many memorable lessons. Sir
Arnold was a master of logic and clear
thinking. His arguments were always fully
developed and penetrating. He taught us not to
be impatient or impetuous. He introduced
us to the art of reasoning. Beneath his imposing
exterior, we knew there stood a man of
humanity, of incisive wit, of warmth and
understanding. He was an intellectual of
considerable stature, yet one who always
carried his scholarship lightly.

John Harker

John Harker, a dynamic and high-spirited
man, devoted most of his teaching career to
making St. George's School, Vancouver, one
of the finest independent schools in Canada.
He was headmaster when times were lean
during the war years of the forties when
money was scarce. Only his ingenuity, drive,
and practical level-headedness carried him
through. I remember him best for his wonderful
sense of humour. He could see the light side of

any situation, and enlivened our days with his jokes. His capacity to improvise was clearly illustrated when he awarded the chess trophy to the winner of the high jump after the high jump cup had disappeared. John Harker was a participator rather than a spectator; he even used to come on cross-country runs with us. He put his distinguishing mark of enthusiasm on everything he touched.

"Cracker" Morris

"Cracker" is currently in his forty-seventh year of teaching at the Friends School in Hobart, Tasmania. He is a living legend. Although he is now over seventy, the years have not dulled his enthusiasm for working with young people. If anything, they have sharpened it. He still conducts the morning assemblies, coaches the girls' hockey teams, is housemaster to the junior boarders, and provides leadership in the classroom. "Cracker" is, above all, an optimist – a man who likes each of the young people in his charge, and has faith in their ability to rise to any occasion. He believes in them and they feel it. Cracker's room at Pendle Hill is a first port of call for countless "old scholars" returning to the school. He seems to have found the secret of youth, and remains as lively in spirit as any of the young people whom he inspires.

John Brown

John Brown is a young Scotsman currently teaching mathematics in Canada. He has a rare combination of technical mastery of his subject, an understanding of the problems his pupils face, and the ability to communicate with them. It is one thing to know your subject thoroughly. It is quite another to be able to explain complicated theories in a manner so clear and simple that even the least able pupils can grasp them. John Brown believes that every pupil is a potential mathematician. His conviction, coupled with his insistence on excellence in performance, touches his pupils. They give him their best and usually end up surprising themselves in the process.

Eileen Hodgson

Eileen Hodgson died last year, but she is remembered by hundreds of young Canadians as one of the lasting influences on their lives. Eileen taught in the Junior School at Lower Canada College, Montreal for over thirty years. She understood boys – she had a family of her own – and helped many of them realize a potential of which they were unaware. Eileen had high standards. She wouldn't let her pupils get away with work or behaviour that was second-rate, and they knew it. Yet in all her dealings with young people, she exhibited such warmth and concern that she gained the admiration of almost everyone she taught.

Eileen had a delightful sense of humour, and you could hear her laughter down the hall on any day. She had, as well, a faculty for remaining calm when others would lose their composure. She was in charge of the other grade six in my first year of teaching, and she gave me advice at that time that has helped me ever since. I'll never forget my final meeting with my own class that first year. I

had told Eileen that I had become attached to
my boys and that saying goodbye was going to
be difficult. Half way through the last class
there came a knock at the door. A boy
entered, carrying a handsomely wrapped package
labelled "To Sir". Inside was a note which
read: "Don't worry. You'll get over it. Eileen."
– and a large box of Kleenex. I don't think the
boys really understood, but I did.

Tek Lin

Tek Lin, a versatile man of Asian background,
is currently teaching English and comparative
religion at the Horace Mann School in New
York City. He is also the school gardener and
his classroom looks like a green house. He
believes in the sanctity of all life – human,
plant, and animal – and his faith in the basic
goodness of things is evident to everyone who
meets him. Tek Lin is a tireless worker, a man
who daily drains himself so thoroughly at his
tasks that he lists regenerative power as one
of the essential qualities of any teacher. He
maintains an open-mindedness which encourages his pupils to express their opinions
freely, and which prompts them to explore
the boundaries of their own minds. Tek Lin
has helped countless young people to discover
themselves.

Thinking about these teachers in order to write
this chapter has rekindled in me fires of
admiration and respect. To all twelve of them I
dedicate these pages with gratitude and affection.

Chapter 8   A Collection Of Poems

The poems in this chapter represent a short collection of pieces written by young people in many countries. They are included chiefly for the enjoyment of readers, although they also serve as illustrations of the models under whose headings they appear. To the pupils who wrote them go my warmest thanks for their inspiration and the joy of the moments we have shared.

Specific Topics

Cobweb
The cobweb is a dust collector
Hanging in the corner.
(P.A., Otter Valley High School,
Brandon, U.S.A.)

Broken Glass
Sharp jagged edges
Glinting in the sun –
Like the pieces of a puzzle –
Transparent and fragile.
(K.D., Iolani School,
Honolulu, Hawaii)

Panti Hose
Many legs this object holds
Eye-catching, short, sexy, fat:
Women try every kind they can –
But they always seem to sag.
(T.J., Scots College,
Sydney, Australia)

Fire Hydrant
Squatting silver in the sun
A solitary mass of metal waiting
for a passing dog.
(P.T., Kamehameha School,
Honolulu, Hawaii)

Graveyard*
Stone beside stone,
Bone beside bone,
Last bed
Of the dead
Grey grave yard.

(J.V., The King's School,
Parramatta, Australia)

Traffic Jam
Honk, beep, go the horns;
Higher and higher rise tempers and voices;
Be you in a Rolls or vintage model –
You just wait 'till the man in blue comes.

(P.V., Raffles Institution, Singapore)

Record
Lord,
Press the switch
That arms the guiding needle
And lifts it from
My plastic back, tic back,
Tic back, tic back.

(D.C., Phillips Exeter Academy,
Exeter, U.S.A.)

Bat
Lord,
I am a bat,
Blinded and I don't know why:
I make my way through countless errors –
Rebounding, swerving from obstacles,
Groping in panicked flight,
Hoping to find a way:
Help me, Lord.

(P.N., University of Toronto School,
Toronto, Canada)

* The King's School, the oldest school in Australia, has recently moved
to a new location in Parramatta where a long-established burial plot
has been preserved in the centre of the campus.

Turkey
Lord,
This is the turkey
Talking to you.
Please give me courage
To face the guillotine.
If I do get it,
Let me end up on
A poor family's plate.

(S.T., Hull Elementary School,
Hull, Canada)

Le Chamois*
Seigneur,
Je suis chamois:
Aidez-moi à sauter
    par-dessus des gros rochers,
A gambader dans les montagnes ensoleillées,
A manger les hautes herbes:
Seigneur,
Il ne faut pas que je me fasse tuer
Par ces vilains chasseurs.

(J.R., Ecole Primaire de Val d'Isere,
Savoie, France)

Tennis Shoe **
Lord,
I'm an old tennis shoe;
I go through mud and water;
My canvas is ripped;
My laces are chewed;
Lord, please save my sole.

(S.R., Beaconsfield High School,
Montreal, Canada)

* translation: *Chamois* (Mountain goat)
  Lord, I am the Chamois;
  Help me to leap over large rocks,
  To gambol on sun-swept mountain sides,
  And to enjoy the alpine grasses;
  Lord, spare me from evil hunters.

** The twelve-year-old boy who wrote this piece produced it in less than
  three minutes in a class that was being filmed live for educational
  television.

Felix, the Führer*
I am no fascist, Lord;
I want milk in every plate:
A home for every animal;
Yet I have one illiberal request:
Exterminate all dogs.

(T.V., Ontario College of Education,
Toronto, Canada)

Soil
Lord,
This is the prairie soil:
Despite all the work I do for men
I'm scorned:
I'm dug up every spring,
And left bare in the fall:
The snow is cold;
But Lord,
What hurts me most is man's remark,
"As cheap as dirt."

(J.W., A.E., Peacock High School,
Moose Jaw, Canada)

Grain of Sand
Lord,
I'm a grain of sand,
One
Among your zillions of beaches:
Yet your touch
Never ceases to warm my soul.

(P.K., Punahou School, Honolulu, Hawaii)

Nature

Dirt
Dirt along the driveway,
Dirt in grubby clothes,
Such fun to mess around in –
To rattle in a tin.

(M.W., Bathurst Demonstration School,
Bathurst, Australia)

* This piece was written by a young Canadian teacher-in-training.

April

April is spring;
April is a wet month;
Mist on the hilltop;
Rain on the roof;
Birds carrying bits of straw;
Shining green leaves:
April is a wet month;
April is spring.

(P.J., Harbour Island Public School,
Nassau, Bahamas)

Birds

They see things so quickly,
Their eyes might burst,
A race to see which one
Will get the worm first.
Their hearts are as tense
As fluorescent lights:
Their brains are bombarded
With myriad sights.

(C.M., Brisbane Church of England Grammar School,
Brisbane, Australia)

The Ice Peak

Right in front of me stands
The snow peak Kachanjunga:
It is a peak that is ever white—
With small black tinges in summer;
Though several miles away,
It seems to stand right below my nose.

(N.J., St. Paul's School, Darjeeling, India)

Cowslip

Swaying cowslip,
Hidden in the moonlight;
Timid under the midnight sky—
In the dew

(J.G., Leighton Park Friends School,
Reading, England)

Bubble
A small bubble of air, frozen into the ice,
Shines among the dark brown streaks
Of the dirty water.

(K.B., Phillips Exeter Academy,
Exeter, U.S.A.)

My Country, City Or Town

Land of golden beaches,
Jagged mountains, upland plains;
Land of hydro lakes and turbines,
Orange sunsets, tourist planes:
Tarmac roads, the sparkling Derwent;
White-capped Wellington crowns it all.

(P.L., Friends School, Hobart, Australia)
title: Tasmania, Australia

On the prairie the wind blows free,
The sun shines at its most:
The pines and maples grow so tall
The sky is clear;
The wheat is ripe–
My country's best of all.

(C.S., Bushell Park School, Moose Jaw, Canada)
title: Canada

From Koko Head to Diamond Head
Subdivisions galore:
From Diamond Head to Aloha Tower,
More apartments do soar.

(F.B., Punahou School, Honolulu, Hawaii)
title: Hawaii

A vast land of black people,
Flowing rivers,
Stretching mountains:
Spectacular continent
Of wild beasts,
Freedom,
Nature beyond compare.

(A.M., Jamhuri High School, Nairobi, Kenya)
title: Africa

Rain pours down;
Mist swirls off heather-covered mountains;
Midges swarm and bite;
Is this the place we've driven miles to stay at?

(J.S., Foremark School, Derbyshire, England)
title: Loch Lomond

Medieval,
Lots of dust,
A famous abbey;
A beautiful mill;
Near the bloody meadow –
Seventy-one is anniversary.

(S.S., Repton School, Derbyshire, England)
title: Tewkesbury, Gloustershire (England)

The sunburnt outback
Shimmers in the sun,
While the foamy waves
Crash over the coral.

(G.D., Brisbane Grammar School, Brisbane, Australia)
title: Queensland, Australia

Name A Month

Lethargy and indolence;
Bushfires and blowflies;
No rain.

(T.M., J.J. Cahill Memorial High School
Sydney, Australia)
title: February

Arrows of birds are pointed south;
Winter's shadows dip through the door;
The orange moon grins through a bare bush.

(J.V., Wagar High School,
Montreal, Canada)
title: October

Everybody's slowed down;
Popsicle puddles on the ground;
Car seat, hot street,
Sunburn, and corn for sale.

(J.L., Phillips Exeter Academy,
Exeter, U.S.A.)
title: August

Mists shroud the valley
And it's damp;
Yet on bright days
You see leaves turning from green to yellow.

(N.P., Repton School,
Derbyshire, England)
title: October

Burnt red backs,
Bright blue sea,
Days that never end.

(A.B., Brisbane Grammar School,
Brisbane, Australia)
title: December

Cinquain

People

People,
Fat, skinny,
Funny, sad, happy,
Always on the go,
People.

(W.D., John Rennie High School, Montreal, Canada)

Footballer*

Footballer,
Boisterous, energetic,
Wet, muddy, slippery,
Shows pink when scrubbed,
Footballer.

(C.N., Friends School, Hobart, Australia)

Pizza

Pizza,
Sausagey, tomatoey,
Hot-sauced, mild-sauced, pepperoni-like,
A tasty flying saucer,
Pizza

(W.W., Otter Valley High School,
Brandon, U.S.A.)

* This poem was produced at a family "write-in" by the mother of a
   lively eleven-year-old boy who is one of the top Australian Rules
   football players at Friends School, Hobart, Tasmania.

Hair
Hair,
Shining, wavey,
Blond, brushed, tidy,
Looks better on girls,
Hair.

(M.V., Downlands College,
Toowoomba, Australia)

Refugees
Refugees,
Small, thin,
Wiry, hungry, shapeless,
They need a house,
Refugees.

(D.S., Jamhuri High School,
Nairobi, Kenya)

Animal Songs

Whale
A king of his environment,
A lazy vagabond
With a brain so big
And logic small-
An invincible power;
He roams the sea.

(R.S., Westmount High School,
Montreal, Canada)

Black-Headed Vulture
Dark brooder
With hunched shoulders-
An undertaker dressed in black,
Ready to swoop
And tear his victim
To fleshy pieces-
Ready to gorge himself.

(J.H., Repton School,
Derbyshire, England)

Dog
She walks with the motion of being free,
With a snobby uplift of the head:
To her, all dogs should have equal rights
To sit on chairs and lie on beds.

(M.R., Dunton High School,
Montreal, Canada)

Set-Scansion Ballad

The Ballad of Lassie the Vanquisher*
And in Suburbia wood one day,
dog Lassie and boy Tim did play;
And they had fun between the woods,
As every boy and dog well should.

But look, tube fan, in yonder grass,
There lurks the deadly snake, alas!
And there, in close-up shot, fangs beg
for Timmy's prepubescent leg.

Oh, what can save poor Timmy's life?
And nowhere is a gun, a knife:
And you the viewer sweats, but knows
That Lassie vanquishes her foes.

In color, snake's head rises high;
Will Lassie pass and let it lie?
She barks a warning: Timmy knows
That Lassie vanquishes her foes.

Her head held high, she circles round,
In one big technicolored bound,
She beats the snake at his own game,
And goes for Timmy's throat, for shame.

(D.P., Phillips Exeter Academy,
Exeter, U.S.A.)

* This poem, written to the specifications of the ballad stanza by the
  editor of the school newspaper, had the following footnote: "Every
  red-blooded American child has watched Lassie, the courageous
  collie, save her master Timmy, from all sorts of danger, twenty-four
  hours a day".

A Sense Of Wonder

Serfin*
wen i wos serfin wun day
i kiwt a big waff i
wos goin buttfll

(J.M., Bathurst, Australia)

Feast **
A broken bottle,
A gutted fish,
An empty can:
The fishermen have feasted.

(J.S., Friends School,
Hobart, Australia)

Sports Car
Warm steel,
Bright sunlight,
Rushing wind,
Dancing hair:
Floating, gliding, climbing needle-
White strokes on black become a blur.

(D.C., Brisbane Grammar School,
Brisbane, Australia)

Paper Glider
Soaring on the currents-
Up and up it flies:
A graceful sweep,
A fantastic curve-
On the wind it lies.

(J.G., Northmount High School, Montreal, Canada)

Deer Season
The crackle of leaves underfoot;
The coldness of the bark of a fallen tree;
A light layer of snow on the cabin roof;
The smell of pine and crispness in the air-
Deer season.

(J.A., St. Johnsbury Academy,
St. Johnsbury, U.S.A.)

* This piece is reproduced exactly as it was written by an Australian boy six years old.

** This poem was done after its writer had spent a memorable two-week holiday in New Caledonia.

What Excites You?

Coffee

Coffee tastes like the roots
  of some wonderously gnarled tree
I once sat beneath,
  whose soil I once sifted through my fingers;
Its steam fills my nostrils
  and my head with peaceful thoughts;
To dig coffee is like being filled
  with soft, haunting music,
  tearing at your soul and
  breathing deep, contented breaths.

(C.T., Carmel High School,
Carmel, U.S.A.)

Selflessness

Selflessness doesn't mean 'without a self';
It means that there are so many selves of you
That you can forget to worry about
  any of them
  and give a few away too.

(B.S., Putney School,
Putney, U.S.A.)

Diet

Fruit cake,
Cream buns,
Macaroons,
Boston buns,
Minties,
Chocolates,
Ice cream,
Biscuits,
I HATE YOU DIET.

(D.H., Cranbrook School, Sydney, Australia)

Appendix
Of Schools

In this book, I have used as examples 318 poems written by young people who are pupils at 105 different schools around the world. I am most grateful to them for their contributions, as I am to their principals for their support. Let me present in this appendix a list of the schools, arranged geographically, from which I have collected these examples.

Canada

Quebec: Montreal and area

Beaconsfield High School, Beaconsfield
Cardinal Newman High School
Dorval High School, Dorval
Dunton High School
John Grant High School, Lachine
John F. Kennedy Girls High School
Macdonald High School, St. Anne de Bellevue
Marymount High School
Monklands High School
Monseigneur Doran High School
Montréal West High School
Northmount High School
Our Lady of Mt. Royal School
Outremont High School
Pius X High School
John Rennie High School, Pointe Claire
Riverdale High School, Pierrefonds
Royal Arthur School
St. George's School, Westmount
St. Ignatius of Loyola School
Verdun High School
Wagar High School, Côte St. Luc
Westbrook School, St. Laurent
West Hill High School
Westmount High School

Other Canadian schools

Metis Beach School, Metis Beach, Québec
Bishop's College, Lennoxville, Québec
Gatineau Mills School, Gatineau Mills, Québec
Hull Elementary School, Hull, Québec
Philaemon Wright High School, Hull, Québec
University of Toronto School, Toronto, Ontario
Ontario College of Education, Toronto, Ontario
St. John's Cathedral Boys School, Selkirk,
    Manitoba
Fleming School, Brandon, Manitoba
Neelin High School, Brandon, Manitoba
Central High School, Moose Jaw, Saskatchewan
A. Peacock High School, Moose Jaw,
    Saskatchewan
Bushell Park School, Moose Jaw, Saskatchewan
Ross School, Moose Jaw, Saskatchewan
St. George's School, Vancouver,
    British Columbia
York House School, Vancouver,
    British Columbia
Shawnigan Lake School, Shawnigan Lake,
    British Columbia

United States

Brandon Graded School, Brandon, Vermont
Otter Valley High School, Brandon, Vermont
Lyndon Institute, Lyndonville, Vermont
St. Johnsbury Academy, St. Johnsbury, Vermont
Putney School, Putney, Vermont
Phillips Exeter Academy, Exeter, New Hampshire
The Phillips Academy, Andover, Massachusetts
Newton High School, Newton, Massachusetts
Belmont Hill School, Boston, Massachusetts
Harvard Education School, Cambridge,
    Massachusetts
Horace Mann School, Yonkers, New York
Marine Military Academy, Harlingen, Texas

Carmel High School, Carmel, California
Iolani School, Honolulu, Hawaii
Kamehameha School, Honolulu, Hawaii
Punahou School, Honolulu, Hawaii

Australia
New South Wales
Sydney and area

Bellevue Hill Primary School, Bellevue Hill
J.J. Cahill Memorial High School, Mascot
Coogee South Primary School, Coogee South
Cranbrook School, Bellevue Hill

The King's School, Parramatta
Loretto Convent, Normanhurst
Newington College
Normanhurst Boys High, Normanhurst
North Ryde High School, North Ryde
Mount St. Benedict's Convent, Pennant Hills
Pittwater House Grammar School, Collaroy
St. Ignatius College Riverview, Lane Cove
Santa Sabena Convent, Strathfield
Scots College, Bellevue Hill
Sydney Grammar School
Wollhara Demonstration School

Bathurst Demonstration School, Bathurst

Queensland

Brisbane Church of England Grammar School,
    Brisbane
Brisbane Grammar School, Brisbane
Presbyterian Ladies College, Warwick
Scots College, Warwick
Downlands College, Toowoomba

Australian Capital Territory

Canberra Grammar School, Canberra

Tasmania

Friends School, Hobart
Taroona High School, Taroona
Howrah Primary School, Hobart
Dalton School, New Town
Hutchins School, Hobart

England

Bilton Grange School, Dunchurch
Crown Woods Comprehensive School, London
The Dragon School, Oxford
Foremark School, Repton, Derbyshire
Henley Grammar School, Henley-on-Thames
King's School, Canterbury, Kent
Leighton Park Friends School, Reading
Repton School, Repton, Derbyshire
St. Edmund's School, Canterbury, Kent
Winchester College, Winchester

Schools in other countries

Harbour Island Public School, Bahamas,
     West Indies
St. Benedict's School, Bahamas, West Indies

Ecole Primaire de Val d'Isère, Savoie, France

Jamhuri High School, Nairobi, Kenya,
     East Africa

Commercial High School, Addis Ababa, Ethiopia

St. Paul's School, Darjeeling, Nepal, India

Raffles Institution, Singapore

Garoka High School, Garoka, New Guinea
Garoka Teacher's College, Garoka, New Guinea

Index